Original E-Book Cover Painting 2001-2005

By the author

Under The Mormon Tree

THE FIRST 50 YEARS

Second Edition

An Autobiography of Mormon Dissident

Douglas A. Wallace

© *Copyright 1999-2006 -2007-2009 -2011-2012-2015*

By Douglas A. Wallace last editing Nov. 17, 2012

Forward

It isn't easy writing about one's own experiences with matters that would appear to be in the category of the supernatural or the "kinky", "kooky" or "Spooky". Yet I have felt for a number of years that my experiences ought to be made available for others to read. The extent and scope of those experiences relate to matters affecting religion. Indeed I have to admit that my life has centered on religion, that is, a belief in a Higher Power. It did in my youth and has carried on to adulthood even if my perceptions have changed, religion then and now has been all consuming of my life.

Being raised as a Mormon that Higher Power took on a specific concept of the mind. Mormons believe and are taught to believe that God is the literal father of Jesus Christ and that he has a body of flesh and bones. In other words, Jesus Christ was created as the result of a sexual act of God, first as a spirit child with a heavenly mother in the heavens and later in mortality by a second sexual act of God with the Virgin Mary. Mormon doctrine goes even farther. It states that God first created man spiritually as a result of a sexual act. It teaches that man, in time, may become a God with many heavenly wives and himself create planets and stars ruling over his own creations the same as God his father has done ad infinitum. That is what my parents were taught and believed. Indeed that is what all Mormons are taught to believe. It is a concept that is very carnal and worldly; in fact downright phallic in nature. Sex both earthly and heavenly with eternal procreation is the underlying foundation of Mormonism.

I no longer believe in such childish nonsense. I continue however, to believe in a Higher Power but I have no concept of what that Power looks like or what form, if any, it may take. I have no concept of the diverse abilities of that Power and certainly no concept of any limitation of abilities of that Power. I simply accept that the Power exists and that indeed all creatures and I are a part of it. That Power has been given many names or titles. In this book I simply refer to the Power as God. The reader can take any personal notion of that power that he or she is comfortable with. So my references to God or Lord in this book are peculiarly my own and not necessarily the notion or view of the reader.

At an early age I experienced a spiritual encounter with that Power wherein I had a conversation about my future adult life. That experience was repressed for many years until long after I had encountered any number of other kinds of spiritual experiences. I was then at the right place and time to regain full recall.

By that time in 1976, I had stepped out of the confining shell of Mormonism and was indeed challenging the leadership of the Mormon Church. The issue, which provided that open rebellion, was the church denial of Blacks in the church's priesthood. It was in the seventies when ball teams were boycotting Brigham Young University ball teams because the Mormon Church owned the university and it reflected the racist doctrine of the church.

It was an easy thing to do like shooting at metal ducks at a circus midway. As a result of that act of open public rebellion against the unpopular restraints of the church, the act gained worldwide publicity. The media picked up on it and the church was embarrassed forcing it to abandon its policy of racism. Since 1978 Blacks have officially been allowed to hold Mormon priesthood but it has yet to admit that my efforts pressured that change.

However that was not the end of the perceived mission of this writer. This book will detail some very sinister aspects of the Mormon Church that every American should be aware of. Those sinister aspects came into focus within two years of the open rebellion of the writer. They were not new to past historical times but were new to the writer and indeed will be to everyone who reads this book and learns of the sinister nature of the Mormon Church leadership or more specifically the sinister element doing their bidding.

I have changed the names of some of the individuals to protect innocence. Where I have done that I have so indicated. The reader may well wonder as he or she reads this story if the writer had it all together. I would ask that you make no judgment concerning that issue. I prefer to leave it in the hands of the Higher Power. What I report happened to me, as I perceived it.

Many former Mormons have reached their own conclusions of the falsity of the church. Some have even gone to the extreme of becoming atheists as they have attempted to unwind the mysteries of the ages and realized that much of what people think and act in regard to religion is based largely on myth and misconception. The Higher Power is not eliminated nor diminished because of individual belief systems, I allow all persons to have their personal belief system regardless of whether it conforms to my own or not. It matters not to me if they are believers or non-believers in God. I have friends in all categories.

As for me I have to rely on the personal spiritual experiences and encounters that I have had with that Higher Power. I seek no fame or glory for that which I encountered and endured. May the reader enjoy this work accepting or rejecting any part that fails to fit in with his or her own psyche.

Faithful Mormons will be discouraged from reading this book and I can understand that as most Mormons are blinded by the claims of founder Joseph Smith, Jr. and by the claims of successive leaders that all is well in "Zion". However, if any one of them has the courage to check out the other side of the coin of Mormonism, they will be blessed with freedom from that prison of the mind for perhaps the first time in their lives.

I wish to acknowledge the invaluable assistance of my sister Jean Patricia Kvavle herself a writer in editing this book. I wish to thank the many individuals who have given me their support and encouragement over the years. Among these are Darlene McIntire, Byron Marchant, Dr. John Fitzgerald, John Evans, Marion Wright and many others who know who they are.

February 7, 2001 Second Edition February 19, 2006-2007 in Reno Nevada Author

Update: August 5, 2009 in the past few years I have learned of the "spooky" issue called the Quantum Enigma where psi or paranormal experiences have been scientifically proven to exist as a contradiction of the laws of Quantum Theories, but with no explanation yet of how they work. This discovery has given me great comfort allowing me to again proceed with public notice of my sense of mission coming from the Cosmos. Only time will prove its veracity.

Behold the turtle! He makes progress

only when he sticks his neck out.

- James B. Conant

Table of Contents

Chapter 1   Some Roots 8
Chapter 2   Some Early Memories 13
Chapter 3   More Early Memories 19
Chapter 4   From Childhood to Adolescence............23
Chapter 5   An Adventure in England 30
Chapter 6   Back In Portland 39
Chapter 7   Mission Home to Mission Field 45
Chapter 8   The Return Home 54
Chapter 9   A Mission Plus One Year........................61
Chapter 10 Into The Crucible of Marriage 68
Chapter 11 Some Spiritual Things............................73
Chapter 12 Two More Years of Academic Delay........76
Chapter 13 The Law Student....................................80
Chapter 14 The Graduate...93
Chapter 15 Questions Of Sanity..............................97
Chapter 16 The Marriage Ends 107
Chapter 17 A New Relationship..............................113
Chapter 18 The Passing of the Patriarch **120**
Chapter 19 A Night Of Direction.............................125
Chapter 20 Busy Bees 128
Chapter 21 Priesthood from the lord 132
Chapter 22 Repression Broken.. 138
Chapter 23 Te Lords Work Rejected........................145
Chapter 24 Excommunication!..................................154
Chapter 25 Opening The Mind..................................158
Chapter 26 Visions of Tomorrow Year......................162
Chapter 27 Assessing The Situation 166
Chapter 28 The Legal Engagement.........................170
Chapter 29 Darlene's Ordeal Begins.......................183
Chapter 30 Some Focus On The Year '77................188
Chapter 31 More Focus On The Year '77.................197
Chapter 32 Subterfuge In Shelton...........................205
Chapter 33 Hughes, Meier And Mormons.................223
Chapter 34 The Cherry Processor............................233
Chapter 35 More Intrigue...242
Chapter 36 Ending The First Fifty Years...................249

Chapter One

Some Roots

Alexander, "Alec" Henry Wallace was born In Westerham, Kent, England in 1896. His father, William Wallace and mother, Mary Jane Jackson had previously given birth to a son, Jack. The couple attempted a failed abortion of Alec. This fact was made known to him in his childhood when a relative blurted it out in anger. Later a sister, Florence was born.

This family was the second family of William. He had a first family from a prior marriage. So Alec, in addition to siblings Jack and Florence, had half sisters Barbara and Janet and half brothers Sid and Bill.

Knowing that an abortion of him had been attempted, Alec went through life with feelings of inferiority. Both his older brother and younger sister were given privileges denied him. School came very difficult for him and he played hooky far too often. As a result, his penmanship was poor, as was his math. Reading was never easy but he did enjoy doing it even if slow at it.

Mormonism came into the lives of the family of William and Mary Jane. They were converted to Mormonism before the First World War. They immigrated to Utah settling in Ogden. The choice of location was likely due to the fact the missionary who had converted them to Mormonism also lived there.

Alexander (Alec) Henry Wallace

Circa 1919 age 23

Alec Wallace as an eighteen-year-old joined the Utah National Guard and was nationalized to federal status during the Mexican Border incident of 1916. He rode as a "Johnny Long Knives" in the cavalry. It was that service that gave him rights to veteran's burial benefit in Willamette National Cemetery at Portland, Oregon, many years later.

Within 6 weeks of each other, William Wallace and Mary Jane Jackson Wallace died in 1917. Alec joined the London Scottish Regiment, being recruited in Salt Lake City. He was en route to England for duty as a machine gunner in the trenches of France when an explosion of a munitions ship in the Halifax, Nova Scotia harbor caused injury to his right knee that burdened him all his life.

He continued on to the trenches and saw duty until it was discovered he was wearing an elastic bandage to keep his knee together. The regiment wore kilts and long stockings so he had been able to hide it. A new sergeant ordered his squad out of the trenches for calisthenics exposing the injury. He was shipped back to Guys Hospital in London, England then, after a questionably successful surgery was discharged.

Alec met Naomi Edith "Edie" Griffin, a friend of his cousin, Susie Jackson, prior to going to France. After the discharge, the couple married in 1919. Both were Mormons, Edie having gone through her own conversion by Mormon missionaries from Utah at the start of the war. In Mormonism, the ultimate earthly quest is obtaining one's endowments* in a temple.

Naomi Edith (Edie) Griffin

Circa 1916 age 18 years

[* Endowments consist of a combination of, (1) the right to wear secret underwear with Masonic markings on them; (2) sworn oaths of secrecy about the ceremony. (3) An agreement to have one's throat slit if he or she reveals the secret**: as well as, (4) additional oaths of total subordination to the will of church leaders. A promise of celestial life in the hereafter is the reward] [** omitted in 1990]

There were no temples at the time in England or Europe so the couple looked forward to immigrating to Utah to obtain those perceived blessings for themselves and their children in a temple in Utah. They were "sealed" together in 1932 in the Salt Lake temple. None of their six children were born under the "covenant" but were sealed to them later.

In October 1928 Alec and Edie Wallace sailed from England to America bringing with them four daughters, Muriel, age seven, Joan, age 5. Marjorie, age 3 and Jean, age 11 months together with a son to be born eight months later.

It was because Alec had lived in Ogden, Utah before that he decided to return there. As it turned out, it was a poor choice. It would have been better for him and the family had he gone on to Oregon where his older Brother, Jack, had first come before the First World War. Oregon is where Alec spent roughly the last 40 years of his life.

Nevertheless, it was Ogden where Alec's two sons were born as well as a seventh daughter who died in infancy. It was also in Ogden that his parents were buried in the same cemetery he buried his last child.

Ogden Utah was a railroad town. The continental railroad that Abraham Lincoln gave vast tracts of land to in the territory passed through Ogden. Mormon main body pioneers had earlier entered the Valley of the Great Salt Lake on July 24th, 1847. It was here that Mormon leader, Brigham Young declared, "This is the Place".

Between 1847 and the 1870's, Brigham Young sent out Mormon colonizers to settle as much of the Utah territory as he could. These settlers were dispatched into Canada; what is now Idaho, Montana, Arizona, Nevada and of course Utah. This roughly outlines what Young considered to be his Empire or "Kingdom of God" or "Deseret" as he called it. Theocracy was the name of the game and Young played it ruthlessly.

Young did not want the railroad coming through his kingdom for he knew it would bring in "gentiles". (Non Mormons) A massacre of a railroad survey party, the Captain John Gunnison Party, at Sevier Lake southwest of Delta, Utah occurred in October 1853 allegedly by Indians. That proposed route would have taken a trans- continental rail line along roughly the route of highway U. S. 50. It was believed by many in Washington, D. C. that Young had ordered the massacre. When the inevitable transcontinental railway did come it passed well north of Salt Lake City.

With the railroad came Asians and African Americans. These people were looked down upon by the white supremacist Mormons. As a result, Ogden, although becoming the second largest city in Utah, was held to be a second class city. Being born in Ogden had the same connotation as being born in Nazareth.

Remembering the scriptural question, "Can anything good come out of Nazareth", one could say the same about Ogden in its early history. As an indication of the lack of its esteem, Mormon temples were built in several smaller communities many years before a temple was to be constructed in Ogden. In fact it would be 100 years after the railroad came before that happened. So it was in this city that I was born in the Dee hospital on May 8, 1929.

Author, 1930 age 9 months

Chapter Two

Some Early Memories

As a child in Ogden, Utah, I recall the hot Summer days and nights; the occasional heavy rains; the wind storms that whipped up the dust blowing down anything too weak to resist it; the winter heavy snows, and the icicles hanging from the eaves.

We lived in a small house at 657-7th Street. It seemed to me that dad constantly remodeled it. At some time earlier, before my fifth birthday, the family lived in a very small alley house between 27th and 28th on Doxey Street for about two years. I don't remember very much except the Chrysler "Airflow" car came out while there. The move was presumably for economic reasons but later, with the family getting bigger, they moved back to the 7th Street house.

Dad was involved with other "saints"" in the business of drying fruit for home use. There was in and about the back yard of the alley house, many wooden bushel baskets and strawberry cups. These items were totally disorganized and in disarray. Often, when returning from some short trip, dad would say, "I've got to get this place cleaned up", referring to the clutter of the fruit baskets.

Always before, "cleaning up" simply meant burning the wood scraps from his building projects. So in my head I thought that was what he meant. Many of my pre-school days were spent on his carpentry jobs and indeed, in my own limited way, had been involved in "cleaning up" his job sites. One Saturday afternoon when dad and mother were gone, I took it upon myself to "clean up" the back yard so that dad would be proud of me when he returned home.

I jumped on the bushel baskets, smashing and breaking them up and started several small fires in the backyard. I knew better than to let the fires get too big. The neighbor came to the fence separating the yards, looking over it in "Kilroy" fashion and said,

"Dougie, are you supposed to be doing that?" My eager response was," Yes, I am helping dad clean up the yard!"

My sister, Muriel, then about fourteen, who was the baby sitter that day, rushed out into the yard with glasses of water attempting to dowse the flames now leaping skyward. Soon a fire engine appeared and the fires were put out.

When dad came home, he applied a razor strap quite liberally to my posterior. The physical pain was more than I wanted to endure, but the mental anguish was even greater. From my point of view, I was being punished for helping my father "clean up" the backyard.

Later, when dad expressed remorse for his conduct, he explained that those baskets did not belong to him, but were owned by the co-operative fruit drying friends. I had destroyed property of others. This experience was a lesson, which a few years later would precipitate another event in my life.

During the two years or so that the Wallace family was living on Doxey street, the 7th street house had been rented, but the tenants paid no rent. When they were notified to vacate, they refused and it became necessary for our parents to take them to court. After court hearings, the renters were ordered to vacate the premises. But before they moved, they went about the neighborhood telling lies about the Wallace family.

The neighborhood was mostly made up of Swedish & Dutch extraction and tended to be cliquish. As a result, a very cool welcome was given the family as we moved back. Only one of the neighbors, Mr. Brewer, a postman, had the courage and inclination to seek the truth about the situation.

As was the case in many Utah communities of the era, a neighborhood was predominantly Mormon. The local Ward House or "chapel" was the social and cultural center for the neighborhood as well as the spiritual house of worship. Most of the children were from Mormon families and associated together both in the church setting as well as in the public school system.

For a very long time after returning to the neighborhood, relations were strained between the local children and the Wallace kids in and out of the Mormon Church setting.

One morning my sisters were sitting on the front porch. A 7 or 8 year old girl from the neighborhood stood on the public sidewalk in front of the house shouting vulgar obscenities at them. In Mormon patriarchy, the oldest male is the protector of the family. I at age five plus, was in that station at that moment and told that girl to shut up and leave, or I would come out and punch her in the nose. She didn't and I did! With blood pouring profusely from her nose she went home crying. Needless to say she didn't bother my sisters again.

Seeing the blood on her lips and chin made me feel sorry for what I had done. Right then and there I vowed I would never again intentionally inflict physical pain on another person.

One Saturday afternoon a week or two before my eighth birthday, I went east, up the street several houses to where some of my boy friends were playing. I went into the back yard only to discover that they had gone through a missing board in the fence and were engaged in an activity which I had learned earlier on 28th street was wrong.

They were jumping on wooden strawberry cups, smashing them and lighting a fire. *Deja vu!* I told them they hadn't better be doing that because the people in the house were keeping them for this next summer's strawberry crop.

At first I didn't go through the fence and was called a sissy. Letting caution go to the wind, I wiggled through the opening in the fence trying to get my friends to quit their activities and get the heck out of there. We all knew that three BIG teenage boys lived in that house.

Suddenly, I heard a hoop and a holler, and turning, saw my buddies going back through the fence opening. I didn't make it before the three BIG boys grabbed me and tossed me into the nearby irrigation canal.

Dripping wet and crying, I appeared at home telling mother what had happened. She called the police who made an investigation and the outcome was that the BIG boys hadn't seen anyone in the backyard except me. My buddies all denied being there and starting the fire. Mother kept me out of school and church for two weeks or more.

It was now May 8th, 1937 my eighth birthday. What a crock to have a birthday and have to spend it at home! Dad had acquired an old chain driven adult type 3-wheel bike earlier giving it to me for my birthday. I rode the machine up the street and went into the same back yard in the hope that I could make peace with my buddies.

They set upon me kicking, punching and telling me to get the hell out of there! I left, got on the tricycle and rode west on the north sidewalk, past our house on the south side of the street. Tears were streaming down my face. My sister Jean was out in front of our house. Jean was always my protector in those early years. She asked me what was the matter? What happened? I didn't answer, just kept peddling on down the street.

I turned north to go to the Lincoln Grade school where I was going to ride on the playground. On the corner, across the street stood the red brick ward house (chapel), the eighth ward. As I went by, I looked at it and angrily shouted, "God I know you are in there! How come those boys can treat me like this and still come and worship you in there? How come?"

Four blocks north stood the two story brick grade school that I attended, Lincoln Elementary. Of course I had been kept out of school while mother demanded some kind of apology from the boys and assurances of my protection from the principal.

Old Lincoln Elementary School in Ogden, Utah

Formerly called the "Five Corners School"

As I entered the playground, to my left I saw a flash of light. I went on forward where I dumped the bike on the pavement. I returned to the location of the light and saw a childlike personage, suspended in the air just behind what I perceived was a volleyball or tennis net. I knew this person, calling out," Michael!"

What happened then became a repressed memory not re-awakened until 39 years later. I was always wondering what had happened and will chronicle my concerns about it hereafter. But this much I will say now. Whatever happened there that day had a profound and subliminal effect upon my life thereafter. The Mormon Church, or rather its leaders, would in the future become an ultimate suspect adversary.

I had a friend, Keith Watanoby, (I am not sure of the spelling) who was an Asian. Keith was pretty much ostracized by the other boys in the neighborhood because of his ethnic background. I was embarrassed that such was the case. Black boys were rarely seen. The Mormon ban on black men holding priesthood always caused me discomfort and embarrassment. It did not seem right to me that God would be such a discriminator of His own creations.

In Ogden, I was far too young to comprehend all the factors by which the Mormon Church adopted the policy of black discrimination. Things such as their being heirs to the punishment of Cain, the brother of Biblical Abel was far beyond my years.

My father seemed to have no problem accepting the policy, for he often would say the Negro race was created by God to be the servants of whites. Most Mormons went along with that notion.

For me it was a matter to be resolved at some future point in my life. Then, and for years to come, it was simply an embarrassment I had to endure but the day would come when I would take forceful action against it.

Author, 1938 age 9 years

Chapter Three

More Early Memories

My father had been a carpentry contractor in England prior to immigrating to Utah. No sooner had the family arrived than the stock market crash of 1928 occurred ushering in the Great Depression. I heard about the lack of work for my father and the need for mother to work for the county as a social services caseworker

Life was not easy for the Wallace family in Ogden, Utah. In the backyard, my father undertook the construction of a nineteen foot travel trailer, a more modern version of the "covered wagon" in which he was going to move his family, now numbering six children with the addition of a second son, Dale, born June 23, 1931.

When the trailer was finished in the fall of 1937, the Wallace family left Ogden. After a tour of several months in central Utah, we ended up on a ten-acre tract of land in Veneta, Oregon, a small community 20 miles west of Eugene, Oregon in the spring of 1938.

Great hope for a better life was present. At the time I recall father having acquired a book titled "Five Acres and Independence" It was his intention to clear the land, plant crops and become self-sufficient. But the proverbial "all year" creek ran dry and the shallow dug well dried up along with it, forcing Alec Wallace to the closest city to find work.

When we moved to Eugene, the local ward of the Mormon Church was busy constructing a church building. Alec Wallace was hired to work on it. Expected of course was additional donation of his time on the building. In the end, many members of his family would donate time including myself as a ten-year-old engaged in scraping off mortar excesses on the brick exterior.

19

During that time Alec and Edie Wallace purchased two tax lots in the suburbs of Eugene not far from the city airport. On these lots, Alec was able in his spare time to frame up a house into which we moved. We used sheets, cardboard and felt paper as wall covering over the wooden studs to give some privacy to the family members. A wood burning cook stove in the kitchen area provided heat for the house as well as for cooking

I remember, seeing the newspaper headline announcing the start of World War Two with the invasion of Poland by Hitler in September 1939. The winter of 1938 was a chilly adventure since no insulation was installed and very little had been accomplished in the way of hard covering of exterior walls, ceilings or partitions.

Over the next two years Alec Wallace was able to get the house into a more finished condition. However, no sooner was that accomplished than Japan bombed Pearl Harbor. Eugene, Oregon was declared a non-critical war defense area, collapsing the building industry.

It was there, in that half finished house, that the "Ward Teachers" of the Mormon Church would visit on a monthly basis encouraging the Wallace family to obedience to the "Gospel Plan" of the church.

On several occasions, the subject of baptism would arise. I was ten, my brother Dale was now eight and my sisters Jean and Marjorie were twelve and fourteen. None of us had yet been baptized. An Older sister, Joan, had been baptized in June 1939 at age 16 while the eldest sister, Muriel, had been baptized at the age of ten in 1931. I remember mother telling the Ward Teachers that she could not afford the white clothing for the children which was required to be worn for baptism.

The age for baptism in the Mormon Church was eight. All sincere and active Mormon parents are anxious to follow the traditions of seeing to it that their children are "blessed" shortly after birth; are "baptized" into the church as soon as they turn 8 years of age and immediately "confirmed" or "given the Holy Ghost" to guide them throughout their lives. To delay these ordinances is to deprive the children of that protection.

It didn't look good for Mormon kids not to be baptized especially when all the other kids in the Ward were. In the end it was arranged for us to borrow some white clothes so that this very vital ordinance could be taken care of. Baptism was scheduled for the four younger siblings on August 5, 1939.

I remember those white, Stout fingers on the hand of Brother Carl Powell as he held them up with his right arm raised in the form of a square. The water was warm as I stood chest deep in it. I also remember the words of Brother Powell, "Douglas Alexander Wallace. Having been commissioned of Jesus Christ, I baptize you in the name of the Father, The Son, and the Holy Ghost".

I remember looking up at the water closing over my eyes (no one told me to close them) as Brother Powell bent my body backwards and sunk my head beneath the surface.

Somehow I had imagined that a miracle would occur, that I might see Jesus or some angel or spirit from the unseen world. None of that happened of course, but I do remember how warm that water felt. Then I thought how lucky! Jesus had to suffer baptism in the cold Jordan!

Up to this time, neither dad nor mom would be seen regularly frequenting the Ward House for Sunday school or sacrament meetings. They did participate in genealogical committee work and I remember many evenings when they would be gone to "genealogical meetings"

I remember infrequent "family home evenings" where there would be some discussion of early Mormon history of the prophet Joseph Smith, Jr. and the alleged persecution he went through. During this time Mother was always doing her genealogical research so that her dead ancestors could be "saved" in the Mormon temples. Dad would be working on the house well into the night, every night when he wasn't away with his regular work.

Bedside prayers were taught us children, but I recollect no training in public offering of prayer. I had heard other kids in the

Ward giving a prayer at the opening of a Sunday school class, but I had never been called upon to do so.

One Sunday morning, Brother Mortensen, as the class instructor, called on me to open the class with prayer. I was terrified and told him I didn't know how to. He persisted telling me to simply express what was in my heart. So,.........."Oh God, I don't know how to do this but I want us all to learn something this day and I hope you will open our hearts and minds to listen and to learn". I didn't remember to say, "In the name of Jesus Christ, Amen".

The next day, a boy from the Ward who had been in that class ridiculed me for not knowing how to offer a proper prayer. "Don't you have family home evenings so that you can learn?" he asked.

I guess for whatever reasons there were; the Wallace family didn't get the usual rote training that other Mormon kids got. Looking back on it in later life, I could observe that the Wallace kids were not equally brainwashed with other Mormon kids, at least not as early on.

Author, 1941 age 12

Chapter Four

From Childhood to Adolescence

Eugene, Oregon is located at the extreme south of the Willamette valley. Indeed the Willamette River enters the valley at Eugene and flows north to Portland providing abundant nourishment to a very fertile valley. The city hosts the University of Oregon, well known for its academic quality.

It was here in this area that other siblings and I attended a four-room grade school, Stella Magladry. I have many memories of those years between the fall of 1938 and the spring of 1942, when the family moved to Portland, Oregon.

Stella Magladry School was named after a benefactor who had donated the site to the school district with the provision that it could never be used for any purpose other than education. Over 50 years later, to this day, it is still used for educational purposes but not a part of the public school system

Next door to the Wallace family moved a family from California. That family was named Stone. The parents opened a gift store at the university. Luther Stone was about my age and indeed a "brain". I found much in common with Luther and we became close friends. However, Luther was treated badly by the other boys in the school probably because of jealousy and their own insecurity. Luther had tediously put together a large balsa wood and tissue covered model airplane. He took it to school for show and tell. The other boys managed to get it away from him intentionally smashing it. This was typical of the treatment he received. In time, the Stone family moved back to California. Stella Magladry grade school did not offer Luther the kind of educational environment he deserved.

A year earlier in Veneta, Oregon I had started school in the fall of 1938 at a rural two-room schoolhouse where four grades were being taught in one room. Because I had missed so much school during the fall of 1937 and the spring of 1938, it was decided by the school principal that it would be best if I repeated the third grade. So when later that same fall I was transferred to Stella Magladry, I was learning the same things and reading from the same books as I had the previous year in Utah. Naturally I was able to raise my hand to answer questions of the teachers quite often. In the fifth grade I was promoted mid term to the sixth grade which was where I should have been.

This simple act of promotion caused a great deal of enmity against me by the other boys in that school, some of whom were 16 and still in the eighth grade. The resentment resulted in my being lured into the outside gym building one day after school. Five or six boys were waiting to take turns punching me. These boys were mostly older and in upper classes.

Deja vu!

Again mother kept me out of school for a few days, while the school principal, Mrs. Gilstrap*, disciplined those boys and made provision for me to return to school. Next year, when I was in her seventh grade class, it became embarrassing that she would rise to protect me from jocular conduct of the others boys in the classroom, or in the hall, when there was really no need for it.

*[*Georgia Gilstrap, about 65 years old in 1940, was a character in her time. She owned a bright green Model A Ford coupe. Students were well advised to stay away from it. In fact she would run out of the school building chasing off students she saw closer than 25 feet to it. One morning she failed to set the brake on her car after parking. Later, it rolled down a steep bank onto the playground and flopped on its top. She always carried a hankie in her hand to wipe up saliva that spurted from her mouth onto a student's paperwork as she bent over the student's desk discussing his or her progress. Though small in stature, she had a big heart with a bull dog face.]*

I want to point out that that there was just two times in my life that this kind of thing happened to me. By and large, I have gotten along with my peers quite well. I must however, admit that what happened at Stella Magladry did influence me to back off excellence in education. I was less likely to raise my hand to answer questions in the future.

One morning, some time later, I was walking up the hill to the school when another incident occurred causing me to tell my mother that I didn't belong in this world, that I was really from a different world.

My father asked me about that statement that evening, while working with him on the house. He tried to give me assurances that this world was real, that I was his son born to him and mother. He missed my point, of course, and I was far too young to be able to intelligently express that feeling. For years after and even today I feel as though I am not of the mindset of this world, and that I truly belong elsewhere. When I speak of "I" it is in reference to the spirit, the soul if you will, not the body.

Notwithstanding the enmity that existed against me among the older, somewhat bigger boys in Stella Magladry Elementary, I did have some boy friends among who were Don Bench, Billy Smith and Dave Gilbert. Dave had an older brother Bob, who had been a part of the group in the gym.

I remember the morning of December 7th, 1941 when the shattering news of the Japanese attack on Pearl Harbor brought me despair. It was a Sunday so I took a walk up the hill to the school pondering the violence that affected America.

It was not long afterwards when dad accepted a superintendent's position on a defense-housing tract in Portland, Oregon. The die was cast for the Wallace family to move. While plans were being made for that move, Dad arranged for the purchase of a building lot on N. E. 72ND Street in Portland which was near the project. The project ran between N. E. Cully Blvd. and 72nd street.

House in Eugene Oregon as it looked in 1994. Alec built this before WWII while author attended Stella Magladry Elementary.

On the property in Eugene, dad had constructed a 24 by 24-foot shop building in which he made cabinets and mill work for the construction jobs he had been working on. I spent a lot of time in there helping him with those projects as well as a few of my own.

One week end in early summer of 1942, Dad came home to Eugene with a farmer friend and his flat bed farm truck. The shop building was cut into sections and loaded on the truck. Now 13, I went back up to Portland with that load and helped dad erect that shop building on the building site he had acquired.

I spent a week inside partitioning off that building so that separate sleeping areas were created along with a kitchen-living area. It was into that structure the Wallace family moved a short while later.

Looking back on that scene by today's standards, it was pure "grapes of wrath". We might just as well have come from Oklahoma and been called, "Okies" I am sure that close neighbors were concerned, if not indignant, about what they saw. However, the structure became the nucleus of a much larger and improved home at 5011 N.E. 72ND Street, which was created over the next three years.

This was of course a continuation of the same method of Alec Wallace. Creating housing for his family first started in Veneta, and then transferred to Eugene. It could be done in those days. Zoning was not in place and building permits and Certificates of Occupancy were a thing of the future. Today it is nearly impossible to do.

I had been very closely supervised by my father in the craft of carpentry and building since age of five. He was a hard taskmaster, and, by today's standards, an abuser. I received both verbal and physical abuse if I didn't do things right. Because of that training, in the summer of '42, it was arranged that I would work on the nearby housing project as a finish carpenter, hanging doors and doing trim. The war had depleted manpower in the construction industry so there were not enough mechanics to do the work. However, it was short lived. Oregon was not a right to work state and the carpenter's union local 206 ordered me off the job or they would picket the project.

They could have examined me and admitted me to the union at that time as a qualified carpenter but because of my age no consideration was given. Besides, my father was not in favor of unions. I did become a member of that same union six years later after examination, at the age of nineteen. However I did continue to work on the project the balance of the summer as a pick up carpenter. I had a partner, the son of the President of the savings and loan association doing the financing. As I recall his name was Guy Jacques, Jr. and he was a year older than I. His father had wanted him to learn something about the building business.

In the fall of 1942 my brother Dale and I registered at the Rigler Grade School. I was in the eighth grade and he was in the sixth. I got into trouble there one noon-time when I climbed a fire escape ladder attached to the building to retrieve a soccer ball that had been kicked upon the flat roof of a one-story section.

Unfortunately, it was just outside the Principals office on the 2nd floor. He saw me through the office window! Needless to say I was summoned to his office where I was given a very sharp rebuke followed by a discussion of liability and law suits, if I should have had an accident and fallen off the roof. I was wrong for doing it, but as I had been crawling over steep roofs since the age of five, a flat roof was a piece of cake.

At the beginning of the school year, the art class teacher asked students to draw a picture of what their summer vacation activities were like. I made a perspective drawing of the framing of a house showing stud walls and rafters. along with sheathing, collar ties and shingled roofs. The teacher definitely did not believe I could have been in such activity, but liked the drawing.

A War Scrap Drive was held one day in the spring of 1943. Students were let out of class to scour the neighborhoods for war production scrap. Before the day was over, we had a pile in front of the school about ten feet high, twenty feet wide and about a hundred feet long. It took junk haulers several days to remove it. During the war years, patriotism was at an all-time high.

In a wood shop class at Rigler. I worked on building a model sailboat for the annual Regatta at the West Moreland ponds. It was to be held just at the end of the school year. My boat was rigged for automatic steering. The boats were released from the east edge of the pond. My boat set out on a very good tracking course. Unfortunately when it was about six feet out, another boat from the right drifted into it both becoming entangled. It took a while for my boat to break loose. We were not allowed to wade out and correct any problems once the start signal had been given.

The finish line had been established as the center of the pond, which may not have been more than a hundred feet.

Boats were then allowed to sail across the pond to be retrieved. In spite of the bad start; my boat was the first to reach the opposite side of the pond. But since that was not the finish line, mine didn't even register. It really disappointed me

In the fall of 1943, I attended Bensen Polytechnic High School, an all-boy school. Boys learned skills that were traditionally male oriented. Girls had their own Girl's Poly or Commerce where they could learn the skills that girls were supposed to learn back in those sexist times. Today Bensen is co-educational and I don't know if Girl's Poly is still around.

Those classes helped to prepare me for a blue-collar job at graduation, since I had no plans for college. Indeed, it was not within the purview of our parents that any of the children were candidates for college level studies. In fact we siblings often heard a statement from our parents that the children of the wealthy went to college only because they were too lazy to get a job.

I took a foundry class in pattern making, which I did not like. A mechanical drawing class was valuable. In fact it allowed me to go through life with a skill that approached that of an architect, when coupled with the hands on experience I had obtained from my father.

I was, however, uncomfortable at Bensen and transferred to Grant High, a co-educational school, before Christmas. I seemed to function better and be happier when there were girls in the classes. By and large I have enjoyed the social company of members of the opposite sex much more than that of my own. It has always seemed easier to communicate with a girl than with a boy.

During this period of my life, I attended church at the Irvington Ward in North Portland on an infrequent basis. Since our parents rarely went to church and then only to "Sacrament Meetings", we kids took a bus and streetcar, with several connections, to get there. Once a day was usually enough.

In the Irvington Ward, I was ordained a "Deacon" and later a "Teacher" in the Mormon Aaronic priesthood. A friend there, Frank Anderson would later leave for a mission the same time as I, and ultimately, we would become father-in-laws to a married couple, my oldest daughter and his son and of course, grandparents to their children. Before that would happen, however, there was a journey that I took which would lead me out of Mormonism.

Chapter Five

An Adventure in England

May 8, 1945 was the day that the war ended in Europe; it was also my 16th birthday. The war in the Pacific would end later in the month of August. I was a sophomore at Grant High School in Portland, Oregon. My sister Jean would shortly graduate from that school. During those eighteen months at Grant, I had taken two art classes and was getting better at watercolor painting.

At the end of the school year in my homeroom, I asked if anyone wanted one of my paintings. I don't remember if a friend, Don Wallace, who sat in front of me, took one, but I do remember girls descending on me. In a flash the paintings were all gone. My homeroom teacher said that she would expect to be hearing about me as a famous artist in the future. I guess I disappointed her. I didn't take up painting again until twenty-nine years later, and then in palette knife oils, for less than two years.

During those high school years, I was expected to take the bus right after school and head to my father's cabinet shop on Sandy Blvd. I worked every day and sometimes Saturday. As a result, intramural sports such as baseball, basketball, track or football were activities I couldn't be involved in. My father relied heavily on me to assist him in production. I can't remember how many chests of drawers I built or trellises or Adirondack lawn chairs.

I wasn't paid a regular wage for this work but was expected to perform as a part of the "Old World" traditions, which my father followed. I was occasionally given some pocket money to go to a movie and, of course, bus fare to and from school. It was embarrassing not to have some money in my pocket as did other classmates, especially when I worked hard and regularly on production of goods. Grant High was at the time regarded as the "snob" school of Portland.

In the summer of 1944, at the age of fifteen, I defied my father and obtained a summer job as a stock room boy at Meier & Frank Co. department store in downtown Portland. I worked in the receiving room on the top floor and was responsible for stocking the fine china and mirrors department on a lower floor.

My dad refused to speak to me all that summer. When fall came and school with it, I returned to the cabinet shop on Sandy Blvd. Dad had rented space from a retired plumber by the name of Burffit, who was engaged in his hobby of wood in-lay portraits in an adjoining shop. Later with father's assistance, Mr. Burfitt built a building east of Parkrose, Oregon where dad had a larger space to do his work. So did Mr. Burfitt. I helped build the building.

I worked in that shop the summer of 1945, as dad had agreed to pay me a regular wage as a part of our reconciliation. It was in that shop the news of the atom bombing of Hiroshima, Japan burst forth across the radio and paper headlines.

During this period of time dad had met a gentleman inventor of a 4-piece concrete building block system. It was a simple method by which any semi-skilled person could build a building. Since the inventor was sympathetic to England in the war, he gave father patent rights to the invention for use in Great Britain.

Upon installing the last item to complete the house on 72nd street, dad threw down his tools and declared the family was moving back to England! The war was over and he thought he could utilize the patent rights to help re-build the bomb-devastated country. It appeared that English building tradesmen had been given deferment to conscription at the beginning of the war with Germany, but were later called into service and most of them ended up on the beaches of Dunkirk, where their regiments were decimated, leaving post-war England with a shortage of craftsmen. It was into this void that dad felt he had the opportunity of his lifetime. So the house was sold, goods were packed and shipped. Then the Wallace family, minus the two oldest girls, Muriel and Joan, boarded a train for New York City.

Because of an over booking of a ship that was to sail from New York, we had to travel to Quebec, Canada where a ship, CITY OF PARIS, was to sail in about four days. The vessel had been used as a hospital ship during the war and was sailing to Glasgow to replace a propeller it had lost. The ship was actually frozen in ice on the St Lawrence requiring an icebreaker to free it for sailing. It was a small ship and broke down in the North Atlantic drifting for a day or two before it could be fixed and under way again. I experienced seasickness during that time. Thank God recovery lasted me a lifetime, for I was never seasick again.

The ship entered Glasgow, Scotland harbor in mid December 1945. Because of British law, I was landed as a British subject even though I traveled on an American passport. We took the train to Dudley, a city west of Birmingham, England where my maternal grandmother lived. We had to change trains and I remember waiting with the entire luggage on the station platform. Indeed this family of six had more baggage than they should have had. So much so that a traveler shouted and asked if we going to perform at the local Hippodrome (live theater)!

We spent Christmas at grandmother's home. I had taken an 18 inch by 24 inch pine drafting board with me, When grandmother saw it, she took it from me and said, "How lovely, ducky that you should 'ave thought to bring me a new pastry board". I didn't explain anything to her, but just let her have it.

It was an experience to meet those relatives for whom I had asked God for six years to protect during the war in my bedtime prayers. Since my prayers did not include relatives from father's side of the family it was obvious who instructed those bedtime prayers.

Author age 16 in Grandmother's back yard

Dudley, England December 1945

Uncle Albert Griffin was about four years the junior of my mother. He spent his working life in radio and later television repair. Mother was forty-seven when we arrived in England so Uncle Albert would have been forty-three. He and his wife Dottie would soon give birth to a daughter Diane. Albert was an inactive Mormon and was what would be called in Mormon lingo, a "Jack Mormon", because he smoked and had a taste for the brew of hops. I was also surprised to learn that grandmother Griffin smoked.

I liked Albert and his wife but never had the opportunity to become well acquainted. After Christmas, the family moved south to Orpington, Kent a small town 20 miles south east of London. It was here that the family would live for the next thirty months. We at first lived in the large home called Gothic House belonging to father's sister, Jenny Barrett. Aunt Jenny's sister Barbara and her sister in law and later her nephew Jack Langford also lived there. So for a while we all lived in that large home.

Because the old house was masonry, it would have made a wonderful prop for the filming of the ADAMS FAMILY. There was a turret three stories high. The kitchen or scullery was way in the back of the house, down a long hallway that seemed like the entrance to a dungeon. The toilet or water closet was in the outside rear of the house also. One would have to carry a candle down that hallway and light gas lamps in order to see.

Central heating? What would that be? Any heat was obtained from sitting directly in front of the small coal-burning fireplace, where your face would burn and your backside freeze. Ice cold feather beds would be heated first by brass bed warming pans on a long handle into which hot coals from the fireplace had been placed, then by crock hot-water bottles. I remember the winter of 1945-46, in that house, as God-awful bone chilling cold.

Probably two months later, our parents purchased a new home that had been built before the war but used as a billet for armed forces personnel. After the war it was refinished and placed on the market. It was in a cul de sac called Lodge Close. A customary name, Glen-Dorrie, was concocted for the house. We lived there until it was sold shortly before returning to the States. Oddly, the couple who later bought it was a Glenn and a Dorrie! It was nice after so many years of living in a construction zone to have a house "ready built". My father's sisters, Aunt Jenny and Aunt Barbara, subsequently purchased a bungalow next door, where they lived after we left.

Being landed as a British subject brought on with it a draft notice to me now approaching seventeen. I certainly did not want to become a member of the British Army for I was a "Yank" through and through. Mother addressed a letter to the Minister of War explaining my situation which was responded to by Minister Bevin, granting a deferment until I would reach the age of 21, at which time I would have to choose my citizenship. As it turned out, that decision was not necessary since I was an American Mormon missionary when I turned 21, even though I was in England at the time.

A very big problem arose for me and for my younger brother Dale. It concerned our education. I was 16 and Dale 14 when we arrived in England. At the time it was traditional in Britain for school children to be basically out of lower education about the time they turned 14. The more bright students went on to college and the potential blue-collar workers went into an apprenticeship to learn a trade. There was literally no public education available for Dale or myself at our ages.

An English couple back in the Irvington Ward had taken us aside prior to our leaving Portland and made the statement, "It is a mistake for your parents to take you boys to England. There will be no opportunity for you to finish your education. They should make arrangements for you to stay here until you have graduated High School." Being eager to take an international trip adventure, I did not bring the subject up with my parents. They should, of course, have considered that matter for themselves. But dad was headstrong, at times, not giving full consideration to the ramifications of all he was doing. Looking back on it, I am not sorry about it, however, for I would not be who I am without that adventure.

My father took me to a public school for commercial art training to see if I could be enrolled. The headmaster there, after hearing about the deficiency of my formal education to fit into publicly supported higher education, which I suppose in England was the classification of his school, said to me, "What is good enough for your father should be good enough for you." I felt like telling him where he could go.

So like the seven dwarfs in Snow White, for my brother and me, it was, "Off to work we go!" While still living at Aunt Jenny's, I began work for a company that made electronic devices. I worked in a department that was responsible for grinding, filing and cleaning up aluminum castings.

My brother Dale went to work at a radio manufacturing company where, as I recall, he continued to work until we left England in July of 1948.

My sister Marjorie was employed to work at a Woolworth's type department store and Sister Jean stayed home to act as house keeper and cook so mother could tramp around England visiting graveyards in her addictive quest of research on her ancestry. Jean was bitter about that and I didn't blame her. It was probably mother's idea more than dad's, as mother controlled the family with her little "ways".

Dad was totally unsuccessful in his attempts to convince British authorities that his concrete block patent would meet their standards. So he gave up on it and became a carpentry sub contractor on public housing projects.

Ironically, the general contractor, E.O'Sullivan, Ltd. had perfected a method of tamped concrete walls which required no forms other than a small hand held aluminum device into which semi dry concrete was poured and tamped to density. The device would be moved along the top of the wall it had been creating, layer upon layer, until the full height of the two story wall was achieved, that system was more in keeping with the traditional masonry wall and was a double wall with a 2 inch cavity between attached together with metal ties. This system also only required semi skilled labor.

Shortly after dad gave up on the invention and went to work as a carpentry sub contractor, he persuaded me to work with him. We were to be "partners" but that was really an illusion. I shared in no profits, if there were any, merely receiving a weekly pay envelope. I did, however, have some independence supervising my own crews of carpenters on the project at Orpington while he traveled north to Sidcup and supervised crews there. In addition to overseeing the framing work on my project, I did, along with another carpenter, attend to the finish work in the houses. This work I kept doing until we returned to Portland, Oregon in 1948.

Author, his father Alec and Brother Dale .Orpington, Kent, England summer 1947

During those two and one half years in England, My siblings and I became more involved with the Mormon Church. The church was still a mission field with Districts and Branches rather than "Stakes" and "Wards". We were in the Catford Branch south east of London, which required a train or bus trip of about ten miles. It was here that I was ordained a "priest" in the Aaronic priesthood of the church. Sunday school and Sacrament meetings were scheduled back to back so that only one trip would be needed. I remember listening to the American missionaries giving their rote sermons about Joseph Smith and the church. I became more aware of the "gospel plan" and the role, which the church was supposed to play in the world.

On the sea trip from Quebec to Glasgow I had met a pretty 16-year-old Canadian girl by the name of Dorothy Ely. Her father had died and now that the war had ended, she and her mother came to England to be near her older sister, who had married an RAF pilot, whom she met while he trained in Canada during the war. Dorothy and I corresponded at first and then I would travel by train on some weekends to visit her. This was my very first romance. She and her mother lived west of London on the underground route at Ruislip.

I made a number of trips there and in between we would correspond. Waiting for those letters to arrive was a lesson in pain! Because her mother and she were Church of England and I a Mormon, it was the first time I had to make a hard choice. Her mother insisted that unless I would agree to reject Mormonism, her daughter would be forbidden to see me again. She did commend me for morality and said she was never worried that I would attempt to have sex with Dorothy when we were alone; that I was respectful and all that but that her view of Mormonism was such that the relationship had to end. Being under the influence of parents and social standing among members of the Catford Branch, I had no choice but to give up the relationship. It was very painful, for I was only seventeen years old.

When my parents had earlier been living in Orpington before their emigration to Utah, my father had converted a carpenter who worked for him, a Charles Dow, who had a family living in the Lee area south east of London, although at this time Charles and his wife were separated. I accompanied my parents up to the Dow household to visit the family shortly after we settled in Orpington. I met the daughter Doris, a green-eyed brunette who looked much like British movie actress Jean Simmons. At the time I was involved with Dorothy Ely so I suppressed any feelings.

Sometime after breaking it off with Dorothy, at mother's suggestion, I rode my bicycle up to the Dow home to see Doris. We hit if off really well. Doris was 11 months older than I, being born shortly before my parents sailed for the States in October 1928.

To make a long story short, In March of 1948, Doris and I became engaged. In July the Wallace family sailed to America returning to Portland, Oregon. It was my plan to earn the money to bring Doris over in about a year so that we could be married. Shortly before we left, Selvoy J. Boyer, the President of the British mission in London wanted me to visit him. He asked me to stay in England and to become a missionary for the church. I, of course, told him my situation and declined his request.

CHAPTER SIX

Back In Portland

The return trip to the States was made on the USS Washington leaving Southampton, England in July 1948. After landing at New York, we traveled by train to Portland. Some friends from the 72nd Street neighborhood had asked us to stay with them while the family made plans for a permanent home. It was a very crowded situation and tensions surfaced. Since there were ten people using a single bathroom one can imagine the stressed situation!

My parents purchased a building site at 134th and N. E. Schuyler where they planned to build a six bedroom Tudor style house, which I had designed while yet in England. Again, pioneering was the order of the day with the construction of a 24-foot x 24-foot temporary shelter on the rear of the lot. The family moved into it. We lived there until the new house construction had progressed to the point where the family could move in and dismantle the temporary structure.

After discovering it was impossible in post-war Portland to work as a carpenter on any housing project, unless you carried a union card, it became necessary for both of us to join the carpenter's union. This was tough on Dad who had a life long contempt for unions but since it was an economic reality at the time, he/we had no choice.

Dad and I went to work for builder Frank White who was developing a sub-division in the southwest hills of Portland. We were doing finish work. However, it was not long before we took on a role of a sub contractor doing mill work and cabinets for the developer, first in a framed house shell in a tract, and later in a large shop owned by the builder.

Within two months after returning to Portland I received a Dear John letter from Doris back in England. I placed a long distance call to her at her work site in London in an attempt to persuade her to hang in there and keep the commitment. It was to no avail.

She broke off the engagement citing the need for her mother to have her support, since she had a young five-year-old brother. I had considered staying in England, so that we could be together, but my parents frowned on it, and I knew that economically it would be better for her and me in the states at the time.

Doris had been baptized in the Mormon Church as a child, but like her parents and siblings, had not had much to do with the church, especially during the war. She told me of so much time, as a child, spent living in the back yard bomb shelter. I would see Doris again some months later, but for the moment had to accept the loss of the relationship with some more pain.

Dad was a restless sort, a "type A" personality, rarely taking the time to enjoy life other than maybe a Sunday afternoon drive. He never engaged in sports or social activities but could always be found working with his hands. He generally sold himself short as a contractor and for that reason would never become a wealthy man. Whatever he gained outside of ordinary wages was obtained by all the extra hours he put into building a family home to get ahead doing it the hard way.

Shortly after the temporary shelter was constructed on the Schuyler street lot, the proposed house was laid out on the site, and then with shovels and wheel barrows, a partial basement was hand dug by my brother, dad and myself. Many years later, it was reported to me that a Bishop of the Mormon Church owned that house and that his son shot dead an intruder in that basement!

Apparently Dad was more impressed with the tamped concrete wall construction, which we had been working with in England, than with the 4 piece concrete block system he had attempted to introduce in England. We built a 12 inch high eight foot long double wooden form system with a separate corner device and proceeded to construct the first story outer walls of tamped concrete, consisting of double 4 inch walls with a two inch cavity between. Thus the concrete wall was 10 inches thick. We went around the entire building, then up and around, layer upon layer. The second floor was wood framed in traditional manner.

This work was done after regular working hours well into the night, with metal light poles giving us the light to work by. Saturdays were always utilized as well. Dad would not work on Sundays. He had an experience in Ogden when he framed up a fruit dryer structure on a Sunday. That night one of those powerful windstorms come through and blew it down. He learned his lesson and vowed never to work on Sundays again!

So little by little the Tudor home took shape. Then as soon as an area was sufficiently constructed, we moved out of the temporary shelter into an area of the house under construction. As I recall, it was the plan to utilize the lumber from the temporary shelter in the new house. Temporary quarters were created in the double garage, from there, we moved into the full house upon its completion.

The Tudor designed by Author at 134th & NE Schuyler

Upon returning to the Portland area my brother Dale, who had only graduated from the eighth grade, was given a special accelerated high school agenda at Parkrose High School, thereby allowing him to graduate in two years. I did not attend school or try to make up any deficiency during this time. I worked to earn money for a mission. I did purchase a lot down the street from where we were building the Tudor for the purpose of building a home for myself, when I should become married. I still harbored hopes that somehow things would workout with Doris. My sisters Jean and Marjorie got jobs in Portland.

One of my sisters, Joan, had become engaged while we were still in England and married upon our return to Portland, The other Sister Muriel, had established herself in an apartment during our absence in England, but did return to living with our parents after the Tudor was finished. Therefore there were the four younger siblings and our parents living in those temporary to permanent housing conditions from the summer of 1948 to the spring of 1950. Well, almost...

After I turned 20 in May of 1949, I asked our ward bishop to be called on a mission for the church. I was interviewed by an Apostle of the church and received a call to the New England States Mission. I was stunned!

I had never expressed my interest in being called to the British Mission, believing God knew my heart and since He would certainly tell our "prophet" there would be no need that I did. So into my sleeping quarters I went and prayed profusely. It was the tradition of expression in Mormonism that when you were called to a mission, where you were called was the will of God by way of personal revelation to the prophet of the church.

There is a hymn sung in the church and at the first meeting of incoming new missionaries into a mission field, "I'll go where you want me to go dear Lord.... I'll be where you want me to be". So powerful was the belief system that to question the location of a mission call was unheard of. This was to be the first time I would challenge an act of the "Prophet".

I sat down and wrote a letter to President George Albert Smith, the prophet and leader of the Mormon Church. I explained that it had been my desire to go to the British Mission, That I had spent time in England and was well ahead of other new missionaries in orientation to English ways and customs, that as such, it should behoove him to change the field of my call to the British Mission, and further, Mission President Boyer had asked me to stay and do a mission there not more than 15 months ago. In about ten days I received a new call to the British Mission. My heart was overjoyed!

While I was waiting for the response to my letter, I was asked by the Ward Bishop to build some cabinets in the Relief Society*Room.

Church policy at the time for such improvements was as I recall, a 70/30 ratio with the ward paying the 30%. I was abhorred by the financial dishonesty that I witnessed in connection with the application for general church funds for the project. The pricing I had given was increased by the bishop to provide the portion that would be paid by the local ward to actually be paid by general church funds. It was the first but not the last time I would witness such dishonesty among the "faithful" of the church.

My dad put an extra "push" on finishing the bedroom in the Tudor which I and my brother would occupy so that I could spend a few nights in it before leaving for the mission field. I wrote Doris and told her I was coming to England on a two-year mission, and hoped that I would be able to arrange a meeting with her. I gave her my itinerary. I was ordained an "Elder" and gave a farewell speech in the Colonial Heights Ward.

Financing for a church mission at the time was the responsibility of the missionary and/or his family. This included transportation expenses to the mission field; all expenses in the mission field including food, lodging, clothing, transportation; as well miscellaneous expenses. The church would pay for the return transportation, provided the missionary obtained an honorable release from the mission. Most missionaries have their way home paid. A few do not. I had saved up enough to pay for at least the first year of my mission expenses. My parents picked up the slack. Later I sold the building lot to help make up the deficiency.

In those days, orientation for the mission field was held in an old house called the Mission Home on the east side of the block on which the church office building stood. It was the first time of my life when Thanksgiving Day would not be celebrated with family.

My first introduction to the seeming mysteries of the temple rites would be experienced. I was personally embarrassed by the nakedness of the "washing and anointing" ceremony; the symbolic blood oath for secrecy extracted from the candidates for endowments; the "signs and tokens" of the priesthood; and ultimately by the whispering at the "veil". Afterward, as I walked across the parking lot behind the church office building toward the Mission Home, I shook my head and asked what was that seeming nonsense all about?

A couple of days later, we missionaries were taken on a Saturday morning guided tour of the Salt Lake Temple where many historic items about it were explained to us. I would again enter that building once more four years later to be married, but for now, while the temple rites did not meet the standard I had expected, I was off on a mission to be of service to the Lord!

[*The Relief Society is a women's organization of the church presided over in the Wards and Stakes by a male person, A male Stake President and a male Ward Bishop. The male Prophet, President of the church presides over it at the general church level. It bespeaks male domination over women under the patriarchal order of Mormonism!]

Chapter Seven

Mission Home to Mission Field

Leaving Salt Lake City by train were 13 missionaries all heading for the British Mission as a group. We went through Chicago and stopped at Buffalo, N. Y. to have a tour of Niagara Falls. Then on to New York City, We were put up in a hotel for a couple of days. It was windy and cold as I remember, so most of the time was spent indoors "studying" the scriptures. I do remember the tour of the Empire State building. All of us had been given blessing by the laying on of hands and set apart as a missionary of the church. We received a certificate of ordination as a minister of the gospel which gave us considerations not otherwise available.

The time came to board the Queen Elizabeth on which we had been booked passage. Leaving home for the very first time was a strange experience for most of us. For myself, I had never been in the company of an all male group for very long and there were some adjustments to be made for this male "clergy" situation.

We elected a group leader, who coordinated our activities. We spent a lot of time studying the scriptures. That was the first time I had read the Book of Mormon from cover to cover. When we weren't eating or exercising or sleeping we were playing table tennis on deck. The ship landed at Southampton and we took the train to London. Mission office personnel were waiting at the train station to take us to "Ravenslea", a large old home in Southwest London used as the British Mission Headquarters, and also the South London Branch of the church.

There were a number of missionaries still in the London District that knew me before I left for the States. Mealtime was the first order of business and then a meeting in which assignments to districts were made. Of course the song, "I'll go where you want me to go dear Lord," was sung. There was some humor when one of the seasoned missionaries piped up, "President Boyer, with Elder Wallace's girl friend in London, I bet you are going to ship him to Northern Ireland!" There was a lot of laughter, as the missionaries coming with me knew about that situation. President Boyer smiled and said; "If Elder Wallace is determined to see her there is no place in the mission he wouldn't travel from."

I was assigned to the Birmingham District about 150 miles north of London. President Boyer took me aside and cautioned me about making visits without his knowledge and consent. Some time later, he told me that Doris had called the Mission office several times the day of my arrival, but that he told her the last time to let me go about my mission. He knew of the breakup, as I had written him shortly after it happened, at which time he also suggested I return on a mission.

Christmas was coming. I was assigned to the Nuneaton Branch with Elder Grant Hardy as my first senior companion. Elder Hardy was a little overweight and wore thick lens glasses. But we related quite well to each other. The Hankinson's were our landlords and we shared the same bed. Looking back on it, it was then customary that Elders shared the same bed. It was not until later, when I was in London headquarters, that I had my own bed.

This practice has been criticized as a factor in the awakening of homosexuals*** within the church. The authorities were either ignorant of the potential or simply didn't care to think about it. The age of twenty is an age when there is intense sexual interest on the part of young men. But the church, for many years, elected to ignore the policy as one contributing to deviation.

*** (See Epilogue for Author's attitude update!)

There was one time when a companion in his sleep began an erotic adventure with me in the middle of the night only to find himself kicked out on the floor! That homosexuals exist within the church is indisputable even among those in high leadership roles.

46

Valentines Day was coming and all of the excitement of it occurred within the branch and the district. A Ball was planned. President Boyer would be there and I agreed to do a pastel portrait of him to be placed on a large heart and hung from the ceiling. A little less than a year later, I found the painting in the attic of Ravenslea in London.

Shortly after the Valentine's event I was transferred to Northampton with senior companion Elder Joseph Brooks. Soon after arriving, I called President Boyer to request permission to visit Doris. He granted the request with the understanding I would take my companion along. So Elder Brooks and I went to visit her.

Brooks asked me to let him talk to Doris first in private and then he waited in another room while I spoke with her. What he discussed with her I don't know until this day, but I presume it was to caution her about the seriousness of my being a missionary. I could not fraternize with females, and that it would be better for a successful mission if she continued her posture of breaking up with me.

When I spoke with her privately she did not yield at all, giving me back the ring. I learned that she was becoming involved with a neighbor's brother, Eric Robinson, whom she did marry and have two children with. Twenty six years later, I would receive an unexpected letter from her from Hong Kong in which she thanked me for having the courage to do the Black priesthood ceremony.

A Salt Lake City real estate businessman, Stayner Richards, shortly thereafter replaced President Boyer. By the summer of 1950, I was transferred back to Nuneaton to replace Elder Hardy, who was being released from his mission with his two years completed. I became the senior companion to two different new elders over the next six months.

Knocking on doors to sell Mormonism was never my cup of tea. There were times when we barley escaped from some people who would charge at us because we were those "damned Mormons". Other times we were treated royally because we were American boys. Most of the time, people had the "bored look," or doors were slammed in our faces.

By the end of 1950, I was called to work in the London head-quarters of the mission as a Special Assistant to President Richards. I was given the title of "Mission Architect" and assigned the responsibility of directing improvements to the church housing situation in Britain.

During the next eleven months, I directed that some dozen branches had chapels improved or furnished them by purchase or by building new. Oddly, The Catford Branch which I attended when living in England over 30 months earlier, was the first to get a new building. I inherited that project, which had been started by another missionary before his release.

Several of the projects involved the purchase and remodeling of existing church buildings. One was a purchase of a synagogue for the North London Branch. It was a real challenge to design the remodeling. It had stepped rows from front to back in amphitheater style, yet I designed a stage proscenium and classrooms at different levels.

Another was the purchase of an old Baptist church built in 1830. It was situated in a weed and vine covered graveyard in the west of England. We tore out the rotted side balconies tossing the waste through side windows into the graveyard. Then we built classrooms in the rear first floor and in the upper level rear balcony which remained. When I say "we" I mean myself, the local missionaries and local members.

Back in London, I received a call from local authorities to say that if we didn't get the mess cleaned up within 48 hours there would be a citation for desecrating a graveyard. Needless to say it was cleaned up! It was amazing to me that the grave yard had not received any attention in 50 years, before we bought it, and no one had cared.

Still another project was the leasing of a site in Wales at Pontypool where the local Elders and local members erected a military prefab. They had dismantled and transported it from an old army post. It was my responsibility to work with local authorities to obtain design approval for permits. In this case, they wanted a steeple. I compromised by agreeing to construct a block tower by the front entry.

Meanwhile, my special status was such that I worked and traveled alone. When at the London office I did share a rooming house with another Elder who was the editor of the monthly publication, "The Millennial Star". actually, then, the oldest continuing publication of the church. For a short time I did have the companionship of an Elder from Boise, Idaho who had emotional problems doing a regular mission selling door to door.

I also was director of the Mission Book Store for a time, organizing and arranging the publication of an all-purpose hymnal for the mission. We could not import books from the States. I also became the Branch President of the South London Branch, which position I held for about six months. I toured, at times, with President Richards and would often precede him in speaking at District conferences.

While traveling with him by train one day to Liverpool, (Future home of the Beattles) where I had a design problem with the local planning authorities concerning a chapel we were converting from a commercial building, he first broached the subject of building a temple in England.

Up to that time, the only temple outside the continental United States and Canada was in Hawaii. There seemed to have been some kind of mental ban on building a temple outside of the Western Hemisphere. Traditionally, the membership build up of the church affected primarily Utah. It was because of the temples being predominantly located there that new converts to the church, such as my parents, immigrated to Utah swelling the population, and hence, the power base of the church. Missions such as the British Mission were constantly depleted of new converts resulting in there never being membership strength to organize Wards and Stakes.

British Mission Office Staff October 21, 1951 Author is in back row second from left with title "Mission Architect"

President Richards requested me to discreetly go about creating a design for a temple and to obtain construction cost estimates. Within six weeks I had created a design which relied heavily on ancient Central American architecture.

The layout was based simply upon my cursory experience in the Salt Lake temple. To overcome long waiting periods between sessions, my design had doubled up the creation and world lecture rooms.

A single Celestial room was in the center of the layout. I did a large 18-inch by 24 inch pencil perspective artist's drawing of the design which I used as a cover sheet. This preliminary design was simply for purposes of cost estimating based upon cubic foot pricing.

In late September, I was in Wales when President Richards received word that his son had contracted polio and was dying. When I returned to the London office, my Temple

plans were missing. I assumed he had taken them with him on his hasty flight to Salt Lake City.

President Richard's son passed away. While in Utah during the October semi-annual conference, we received word that he had been "called" to be an assistant to the Twelve Apostles.

There were two "sisters" (female missionaries) on the secretarial staff at Mission headquarters. They lived in the home of the Mission president and his wife a short distance down the street from Ravenslea.

Elder Grant Bethers, whose title was Mission Secretary, was responsible for all of the logistics of administering a mission field. A Rhodes Scholar, he had arrived in England about a month before I had. Since both of our two-year missions were soon coming to an end, these sisters arranged to have a farewell party for both Bethers and myself in the Mission President's home.

One evening, in mid October, we were in the middle of this party, when the front door opened and in walked President and Mrs. Richards. They had flown back to England and taken a taxi home without alerting those of us in Mission headquarters. Great shock was registered on his face to see this fraternization of sisters and Elders in his own home. His personnel secretary, one of the Sisters, quickly recovered and explained that this was a farewell party for Bethers and me.

With a twinkle in his eye, he looked at me and said, "Well, Elder Wallace may not be going home for a while". He asked me to follow him into the den where, after being seated, he began. "I have presented your plans for a temple in England to President David O. McKay. He has given me a go-ahead to do some further study and locate a site on which it could be built. I would like for you to extend your mission long enough to accomplish this work."

Although honored by this request, I wanted to get back home and expressed concern that my brother was serving a mission at that time as well, and my parents had enough to do supporting him; that they had expected me home as scheduled by the first of December. I told him I would proceed to do what I could and would "play it by ear".

He instructed me to communicate with Arthur Price, the In-house architect of the church in Salt Lake City. Arthur, an elderly Englishman, had conceived the idea of using projection cameras on a blank wall to depict the different scenes used in the temple indoctrination ceremony. I did so and then modified my design.*

[*The basic preliminary plan of Arthur Price was subsequently used in most all temple construction after the Los Angeles temple.]

With a sudden sense of urgency, I placed an ad in a London newspaper. "WANTED, AN OLD ENGLISH FAMILY ESTATE OF TEN OR MORE ACRES WITHIN A 20 MILE RADIUS OF CENTRAL LONDON. CASH WILL BE PAID FOR AN ACCEPTABLE SITE".

I received several responses from estate agents. After reviewing them, I selected three and presented them to President Richards. He in turn picked out one and we made an appointment to tour it. After the tour, I arranged the purchase of an option for it. In the meantime, I had met with two large contractors in the London vicinity and after viewing the preliminary plans, came up with "ball park" figures giving us an idea of what the total package might run.

I had accomplished this within the time remaining for my mission and was thus able to obtain an honorable release and head for home. There was a time frame on the option which required an immediate presentation be made to the First Presidency. President Richards instructed that I should fly to Salt Lake City with the materials and make a positive presentation to David O. McKay. He dictated a letter that his secretary typed. It instructed me in every step of the presentation.

Early in the month of December 1951 I flew in a commuter plane to Glasgow where I boarded a Scandinavian Airlines System Constellation (4-engine propeller aircraft) for non-stop flight to New York City. I remember the constellation pilot doing a standard check out of the engines by "rev-up" at the east end of the runway at dark. The pilot determined that one of the engines wasn't functioning properly and returned to the gate. We were put up overnight in a local hotel while a new engine was flown in from Sweden and installed.

In the morning, we took off. The runway ended at the abrupt meeting of land and water as we climbed out over the Atlantic Ocean. . Those were the days of propeller driven aircraft. It would be several years before the first commercial jets would be in service. In addition to it being the very first time I had flown, it was also a great feeling to be free of the restrictions on fraternization. One of the beautiful Blond Swedish stewardesses spent a great deal of her spare moments seated next to me. We talked for several hours.

The flight to New York took around nine hours. I had to take a taxi into the city to spend a night in a hotel that was paid for by SAS due to the delay in flight from Glasgow.

The next morning I was on my way to Salt Lake City and my meeting with The President of the Mormon Church. I wondered what it would be like. Would he perceive all my imperfections? Would my mission to present a very significant milestone proposition in general church development, fail because of those imperfections? A lot was depending on this twenty two-year-old now ex-missionary.

Chapter Eight

The Return Home

The next morning I was presented to President David O. McKay by the chairman of the Church Building Committee. It was a tense moment as I was seated to the left of McKay at his office desk. Quickly scanning over the drawings of the building, which I had prepared together with a site plan and information on the old estate that was under option to purchase, he asked me a few question attempting to determine if the site was elevated. I assume a promontory view would have been preferred. However my response was that it was not elevated but that along the easterly boundary a train track existed so that passengers would have a view of the site.

My impression of President McKay was "Wow!" he is so old and feeble with his hands shaking. He had only a few months earlier been ordained President of the church upon the death of George Albert Smith.*

During that meeting, First Counselor, President J. Reuben Clarke came in. He too was old and feeble. I was introduced to him as the young Elder who had worked up the British Temple idea under Stayner Richards. I remember the latter's comment "We need to get Brother Stayner back here as soon as possible."

*[President McKay was 78 years old at the time and lived almost 19 years longer, dying at 97 years of age]

President McKay gave approval of the idea with instruction that a telegram be sent to President Richards telling him to exercise the option. I was dismissed and my mission was now really over.

I kept the proposal for a temple in England a total secret for a year or two until it was announced that a temple would built at Bern Switzerland and another in New Zealand, both before the London Temple construction was announced.

It appeared that the owners of the estate that we had obtained an option for in London learned of the purpose for the site, and refused to honor the option. It became necessary to locate a different site further south with the same concept (An old English country estate).

That together with British red tape allowed other members of the Council of the Twelve to push ahead and get a temple built in their respective mission fields before the London Temple could be built. But the barrier had been broken,* the church would become a truly world wide organization with Stakes and Wards to replace what before had been missions siphoning converts to Utah.

Years later, I was glad the first plan failed so I did not have to face up to a fulfilled participation in a scheme that deludes Mormon members into a belief there is anything meaningful to the whole concept of temples.

*[This is an example of how the church works despite the deceptive concept that the President of the church has personal revelation from God on such matters]

Leaving Salt Lake City the next morning, I flew to Portland where my parents were waiting to greet me. A girl that I had dated before the mission and corresponded with during the mission, Marilyn Jolley, was with them. Marilyn was a fine girl and there were times later in my life that I had regrets about not having continued a relationship with her.

Stake conference was coming up, along with it the duty to give my mission report to the local members. Frank Anderson, with who I had been associated as a teenager, the future father in law to my oldest daughter had returned home from his mission as well, and gave his report at the same meeting.

During the Christmas holidays, I received a call from Howard McKean, the church Building Committee Chairman He had been a life long friend of Stayner Richards and was the individual who presented me to President McKay. He asked me to work for the

Church Building Department in Salt Lake City. I was elated and accepted a job.

My father had been planning on me returning to work with him. He had made arrangements for the construction of a speculation house. He was still doing the cabinets and mill work for Frank White, but wanted to branch out.

My acceptance of the church job greatly disappointed him. He attempted to dissuade me with arguments that I wouldn't be making as much money as I could with him. I realized that, but my attitude was that being in the service of the Lord was more important to me than money.

The first week of January 1952 saw me at a desk on the fourth floor of the church office building at 47 East South Temple. Since the church building Department was a part of the Presiding Bishop's office of the church, I was taken into Bishop LeGrand Richard's office for introduction. Brother McKean, head of the Building department, told him that Stayner Richards didn't want me to leave the British Mission. I remember Bishop Richard's response; "Well missions have to come to an end".

I was assigned to be an assistant to Julian Cannon, of the more recognized Cannon family of the church. Julian had, along with Paul Woodruff; another recognized Mormon family, both of whom were registered engineers, gone to work for the church upon graduation from college. He, in fact, both of them never had a different employer until they were both forced into retirement when they turned 65.

At the time, Julian was 46 and I was 22. We had many break/lunch room conversations. I could not help but detect his dissatisfaction with many things that occurred within his purview.

Julian was in charge of the department that took responsibility for lower end cost construction and furnishings items for Wards of the church. Building improvements, refurbishing, maintenance and replacement items were his responsibility up to a certain cost platform.

I worked at a desk adjacent to his and handled a lot of mundane matters, giving authorization for purchases of numerous church pews, chairs, carpets, cleaning items, etc. Because of my skills in drafting design, I would be assigned to go out to wards to meet bishops and go over with them, their wish lists for remodeling improvements. I would then come back to the office and draft up a proposal to be negotiated until agreement. Julian would grant the authorization for expenditure.

Sometimes I accompanied Arthur Price, the church Architect, on his journeys, which were of a higher cost caliber. He worked in the new construction section of the Building Department. As such, I assisted him in obtaining measurements and elevations of construction sites. He and I had good rapport. I often mentioned to him that I probably should go to school and become an architect. His response was "what for? You already are!" Then further, "The only reason you would need to do that would be for credentials."

I attended the Institute of Religion at the University of Utah campus for church services on Sundays. It was convenient for me. I met a girl there, Jackie Anderson, then about 19 whom I dated a few times, even visiting with her family one week end in Richfield, Utah as I had to take a survey of a request from the ward Bishop for improvements to the Ward House.

The trip down from Salt Lake City was made on a Saturday in February. Jackie, of course, was with me. I was driving a '50 black Plymouth in light snowing conditions. In Provo a flat bed pickup truck swerved in front of me at a traffic light. There was no way I could stop. When I hit the brakes, I skidded into the rear of the truck, buckling up the hood of my car and smashing in the grille. Police cited me for failure to stop! It was with that grotesque sheet metal work that I appeared at Jackie's parent's home. What an embarrassment!

Another embarrassing moment occurred as a result of a question that I asked Jackie's father. Passing a gypsum plant north of town, Jackie had mentioned her father worked there. I asked him what he made there, intending to find out what products were manufactured. With a quizzical look on his face, his response was," $2.78 an hour" I stumbled over myself excusing my framing of the question.

On the way back to Salt Lake City, I gave Jackie what is known in Mormon lore, "A Four in One Combination". That means a King James Bible; a Book of Mormon; a Pearl of Great Price: and a Doctrine and Covenants all bound under one cover. These are the "Standard Works" of the church, the scriptures, which guide the belief system and affairs of the church. .

I had the book gold engraved with her name. We got into a discussion about the church and religion in general. At that time Jackie had come to the conclusion that Mormonism was a joke; a fraud if you will. It was an incompatibility that I could not handle then. Years later I would have to admit to myself she was right at that tender age! She did keep the volume out of respect for me I guess. We did not have much to do with each other after that time.

Grant Hardy, my first missionary companion in England, had come home to Salt Lake City and married his girl friend, Janal Clayton. They wanted to have a dozen children, but I don't think they did, although they approached it! I was invited over to their home in a co-operative housing project for dinner one evening. The intent had been to have me meet a sweet girl, who played violin in the Utah Symphony as did Grant. The scheme got messed up because they invited another returned missionary as well, who, being more aggressive than I, was able to drive the girl home afterwards!

Grant and I, while the best of friends at this time, became estranged in later years. We grew apart in our understanding of Mormonism, as I will detail later.

Working for the church was a sensitive issue when it came to compensation. There was no standard of compensation among the employees. Each employee would have different pay not based upon skill or tenure, but more upon political considerations.

When the sealed monthly pay envelope was passed out to us, it had printed on it in 14-point print. "Your salary is a personal matter between you and the Presiding Bishop, Do not discuss your salary with fellow employees."

Negative discussion about it did happen in the lunchroom despite that warning. Some employees, who had been there for years with great seniority, were paid less than some who had recently come aboard. My monthly salary at the time was $300.00, less than half of what I could have been making back with my father.

There was a whole group of "camp followers" lobbying our office from the outside world. Salespeople for different commodities were given preferential treatment. Their bids and pricing were chosen over more competitive bidders. It was a phenomenon I did not understand. Julian advised me that the reasons were political.

Next door to the church office building on East South Temple, was the "LION HOUSE", the original home of Brigham young and his many wives. In the basement was a cafeteria where hot meals could be purchased. A number of times there at lunch, I ran into individuals who had a dissident attitude about the church, airing their grips about one thing or another.

I had never been in that situation before and found it discomforting. I could understand in later years why some family, old friends and Mormons in general prefer not to associate with me. The challenges I made to the "Brethren" and to their system starting in 1976 bothered them.

This introduction to inside financial dealings of the church would not last very long. One morning In March, I received a telephone call from my mother who informed me that my father had suffered a heart attack.

This brought my work at church headquarters to an abrupt halt. After taking a leave of absence; I headed home to take care of father's business. I would never return to that job.

Chapter Nine

A Mission Plus One Year

Dad's heart attack occurred as a result of his raising, by himself, a twelve foot high section of wall at the entry hall of the home he was building. This was the speculative house he had planned to build with me. Even though I had gone, he proceeded with his plan.

The nature of his attack was such that had open-heart surgery been a technique of the day, he would have been able to survive nicely and go about life as usual. Mother had opened a clothing store in Woodland Park, a small community between the Tudor house and Portland. The venture was not successful, and in time she would have to abandon it.

In the meantime, I did what I could to keep dad's business afloat. I had not received any training in business and I made plenty of mistakes that first year.

The first challenge came when Frank White's nephew who had come to work for Frank before I went on a mission was now supervising Frank's projects. This nephew, seeming to take advantage of dad's illness, wanted to cut out dad as a subcontractor and do it himself. In time the cabinet shop was closed and I proceeded on my own to design and construct houses.

Dad's health did not improve greatly and he would have several attacks over the next 10 years. Adjustments had to be made. The Tudor house was eventually sold, and for a time, my parents lived on some acreage in Boring, a small community south east of Portland, where they attempted chicken farming. That situation was more than they could handle.

Eventually, they slowly went through another project by acquiring an abandoned house east of Portland on Glisan Street, which his restlessness allowed him to remodel. He managed to acquire some more acreage in the McMinnville, Oregon area, where he again attempted to build a house.

He had it just about framed up when another heart attack struck. That property was sold and later, he built another house east of Gresham, Oregon where he ventured into the raising of Fuchsias. This project was not financially successful.

Still later, he built another house at McMinnville near my Sister Jean's home. That home was completed not too long before itchy feet caused him to move to Logan, Utah near his sister "Flossie", where he again got into the remodeling venture on an old house.

He was at this time 72 years of age. Two years later at age 74 he and mother moved back to Oregon settling in Salem, where my sister Jean and her family now lived. This time my parents arranged to have a home built next door to the Salem Stake Center/Ward House of the church. It was in this home that he went into heart failure at age 79.

Upon returning to Portland in March of 1952 after just a little over two months working for the church in Salt Lake City, I was thrust into the role of being a provider for dad and mother. I did not like the responsibility, nor was I trained or prepared for the financial aspects of it.

The house which dad had started was finished and placed on the market. When it sold the profit was not as great as it might have been, had I kept better records of its cost when establishing the selling price. I later designed and built two more homes on the same street. They in turn were sold producing a better profit.

During this time, I also started building small starter homes on the FHA 201d program. These homes, including a lot, were sold at $2,995.00 for a 2-bedroom and $3,995.00 for a 3-bedroom. It is hard to consider such prices, when forty years later a fancy pre-hung double front door unit is costing as much as $7,000.00.

The thought in Mormonism is that a missionary within a year of returning home will be married. I don't know if that is the result of being sex starved during his mission, or the carry over of missionary purity when he first comes home. The only honorable way to enjoy sex is to simply get married. This, of course, the church encourages. Marriage and having babies is the basis of Mormonism.

My sister Jean at a ward Mutual night (MIA) introduced me to Pat Ferguson in the spring of 1952. Pat had been the Portland Stake Gold and Green Ball Queen the previous year. I had seen her picture in the Stake News that was sent every month to the missionaries in the field.

Pat was an RN and recent convert, but was very thin and didn't interest me at the time. Our family doctor, George Taylor, also a Mormon, encouraged me some time later to date Pat. He said she was his scrub nurse in surgery and a very fine person.

After dating a few other girls, I began dating Pat. It seemed she had put on some weight. Her face filled out and was more attractive. We had a lot of chemistry, but that was not enough so I quit dating her.

In the summer, I traveled to Eugene Oregon where I met a girl about 19 named Abby Riggs. Abby's family had recently converted to the church. Her family were farmers raising string beans in the country north of Eugene. I traveled there every weekend. She, her sister and brother rented an apartment in Eugene, where they all had jobs. I fell for Abby and bought an engagement ring. She spurned it.

She went back to BYU in the fall. When I went to October conference of the church her sister rode with me to stay with her for conference. At the campus dorm after dark, Abby saw me at the curb from the dorm window. She came running out in a robe to hug me. I dated her once more while in Utah for conference.

I stopped in for a visit in the church Building Department. A girl, who worked there, had introduced me to Jackie Anderson* earlier that year. She asked me to make contact with Jackie. I did and had a tentative date. However my interest in Abby was greater and I canceled the date.

In late October, the Portland Stake conference was held. Sitting in the rear of the gathering, I noticed I was directly behind Pat. After the meeting we talked and started dating again.

About a month later, returning from a date, at her front door in a moment of jest I said, "What would you say if I asked you to marry me?" She threw her arms around me saying, "Oh yes!" Now I didn't mean that question to be a proposal!

I was trapped! Honor demanded that I accept responsibility for my conduct. Besides, my year at home from the mission was nearly up and after all, maybe it was appropriate to follow tradition!

Marriage in the Salt Lake Temple was set for January 6, 1953 with a reception to follow a week later in Portland. In December I had a telephone call from Jackie* in Salt Lake City. She wanted us to get back together. I had to tell her I was now engaged. With a crack in her voice she wished me well.

*[48 years later I had the opportunity to meet Jackie again. By that time she had retired from a career as an alcoholic counselor for the Veteran's Administration. She had never married. Over the years we had grown in entirely separate directions. While she continued to believe the Mormon Church was totally wrong as I now did, we had very little left in common]

My sisters, Marjorie and Jean were attending BYU at this time. They had come home for the Christmas Holidays. So after the first of the year they rode with Pat and me to Utah. We took them directly to their BYU Dorm returning to Salt Lake City where we secured two adjoining motel rooms on the evening of January 4th.

Since Pat had not been though the temple before, it was necessary for her to take out her own endowments. This we did on January 5th. It takes several hours for this ceremony, so I went through for the second time doing vicarious work for the dead. That is, I went through the temple as a dead person. The second time made no more sense to me than the first time 4 years earlier.

My sisters, Jean and Marjorie, having previously obtained their endowments, came up to be present at the temple wedding the next day. They spent the night with Pat in her motel room.

The next morning I awoke deathly sick. This sickness was something that would randomly attack me from time to time, perhaps 5 to 6 times a year. It began when I was around eleven years of age. According to stories related by dad, his mother had suffered migraine headaches, so this malady was accepted as just that. No medical diagnosis was ever made of it, although I had, upon returning from the mission, sought answers from Dr. George Taylor.

Years later, he was to finally diagnose it as Meneares disease. At this time, however, it was held to be a migraine headache. Symptoms of the malady included dizziness, vertigo, vomiting together with pitching and helplessly falling when getting out of bed. Staying in bed with my head fixed in the pillow in darkness was the only comfort. If I moved my head at all, spinning and disorientation would occur. The same thing happened if someone spoke to me.

What a situation!

Some hours later, in the afternoon, I was able to get sufficient control of myself to go for the marriage.

Those who have been married in a Mormon temple will understand the nature of the ceremony. Deborah Laake in her book *SECRET CEREMONIES* details it quite well. Only members of the church in good standing who have their endowments are allowed to be present and witness the event.

After the ceremony, we were walking down a corridor with a temple worker. I was asked if I wanted to have the honor of throwing the big open switch turning on the electric lights which illuminated the exterior of the building. Shrugging my shoulders I accepted and threw it. Big deal!

Pat and I drove my sisters back to Provo and BYU before returning to the motel. I was now nearly 24 years old. Pat was the very first woman with whom I had ever had sex! It can be done, but at what cost? Deborah Laake explains the difficulty of becoming married to a man that has never had sex. Ignorance reigns high. With it frustration of the partner, surely asking if that is all there is to it. If the partner has previously had sex with someone with more experience, of course frustration can be greater. This issue is a dilemma facing the church.

One of the arguments presented for supporting polygamy relates to the basic question of the purpose for sex. By fundamentalists, the purpose is solely for procreation (or so they say). That argument is further supported as justification for a man having several wives.

The fault of that argument of course, lies in simple ignorance of female biology and need. Mormon men, and for that matter any man raised in strict adherence, to a code of morality, is ignorant and inexperienced in the art of love making. They have the urge for sex but suppress it when getting heated in a situation of necking with a girl.

Not understanding that girls have a longing for sex equally strong as that of a man; the young Mormon man is crushed between the jaws of a vise. On the one side is the strict moral code on the other is his overwhelming sex drive. Obeying the rules can be hell!

When there is a discovered violation of the moral code, he can expect to be publicly humiliated by excommunication from the church on moral grounds. This has happened to many missionaries in the field. However, many Mormon men never get caught.

It is easy to see how Joseph Smith, Jr. came up with justification for polygamy to satisfy his own sex drive. All Mormon men who have practiced polygamy have done so for the same reason. In this way, sex becomes a daily delight, not ever interrupted by pregnancy, menstrual cycle or staleness of the partner.

The day after our wedding, Pat and I decided to go to a dinner movie theater in Sugar house, a suburb of Salt Lake. I called my mother and father notifying them of the marriage. I asked Dad how things were going with work. He responded with some negative comment.

After the conversation Pat asked me if there was a problem. I told her there were some financial problems with the business and dad was depressed. We had dinner that evening before going into the theater.

About half way though the film, I sensed some change in Pat's mood. She became stiff, silent, inattentive as well as unresponsive to my arm around her. After the movie, we walked out to the car in total silence. I opened her door and got in myself. Looking at her I asked what was the matter? Then began a verbal tirade that prefaced the next twenty years of my life.

It seemed Pat had assumed the Wallace family was wealthy because of the Tudor home in which we lived. Although at the time I was building a house for us to live in, she knew I had no wealth and worked for wages. I discovered money was at the root of her decision to marry me.

What a dilemma! I was now married for "Time and all eternity" to a woman who was not in love with me. And to make matters worse, I married her out of a duty to honor a commitment that I trapped myself into! I determined to make the marriage work. There was too much at stake here. Besides honor, there was family, friends, the church and God to consider. Paul had his thorn of the flesh (which some writers have suggested was homosexuality) and now I had mine!

Chapter Ten

Into The Crucible of Marriage

Pat and I returned to Portland a couple of days later. It had been arranged for a wedding reception to be held in the women's Relief Society room in the basement of the Colonial Heights Ward chapel. This was held about two weeks after the marriage. This was a social event more in keeping with societal manners than my desires. The Colonial Heights building was a large, somewhat Tudor style structure. It had a lot of atmosphere and charm.

Had it not been for the disagreements that Pat and I were having since our marriage, I would have enjoyed the event much more. It seemed to me to be dishonest. I let everyone believe that ours was a happy match.

One morning about a week after our return from the temple, dad asked me how I liked married life. I told him that if what I had was "marriage" I didn't want it.

I want to point out the fact that Pat and I had a very rocky marriage. In retrospect it would have been better for both our psyches had we divorced upon returning to Portland.

It would be very boring to listen to endless details of the strife that occurred for 20 years. I will spare the reader that trip. It was a roller coaster ride from day to day. I did the very best I could to maintain an upbeat attitude about life. Without question, ours, along with the five children to be born to the marriage, was a secrecy of silence. Friends at church had little or no idea that it was a bad marriage.

Within six weeks of our wedding, we learned that Pat was pregnant. Our first daughter, Teri, was born on October 6, 1953. The second daughter Cynthia on May 11, 1955. A third daughter Jennifer was born on August 4, 1965. Two sons were also born in between: Jim on August 1, 1957 and Kevin on August 19th, 1960.

To critics who would ask why bring children into a sick marriage, I can only say that these children were a delight and are fine upstanding human beings. Perhaps having to endure what they did gave them a strength of character they would not have obtained in any other way. I do not believe there are any real accidents in this life, but there is a reason for every thing that happens to us.

Between January 1953 and November 1963, I continued building houses and some light commercial. It seemed I never learned the lesson of capitalism! Dad had instilled socialism in me, and it got confused with my notions of Christianity. I gave of myself by over-estimating my ability and under-estimating my time and costs. There were a lot of clients who benefited from this. I built structurally sound; in fact too sound. Hidden behind the paint and floor finish was an over-built structure. My competition, of course did it in reverse. They made money and I didn't.

I am sure this had a lot to do with the difficulty of my marriage. Had I been highly successful financially, I often wondered if Pat would have been a true partner and not pulled against me all those years. My children had all the basics but not the extras. That fact caused determination on the part of some of them to seek the "good life" when they were on their own.

In addition to that underlying socialistic behavior, I had an undefined feeling that the day would come when I would be at odds with the Church leadership. That feeling came from the repressed event on the Ogden Grade School grounds on my eighth birthday. I had asked Pat, before the marriage, if she would support me if I had to do something extreme. Her response was, "like what"? Not knowing what it was that bothered me, I had made the statement, "Like going to the most Northern part of Alaska". "Oh yes", was her response. Not too good huh? Since I couldn't say what it was, that was the most extreme thing I could think of.

My lack of a High School diploma was another source of inadequacy for me and an embarrassment for Pat. I attempted to attend an evening adult class the summer of 1960 in order to make up the deficiency. That didn't work. I often couldn't make the six p.m. class time due to ornery concrete that wouldn't set.

I decided to go for the General Educational Development test (GED) in the late spring of 1964. That I passed with flying colors. A fellow who I had built a house for took the test that day with me. We were both a little embarrassed to see the other present. Explanations for reasons why neither had a high school diploma were exchanged. In his case, he had enlisted in the military when he was sixteen. My case had to do with the first trip to England.

Having passed the GED, my next thought was what to do next? There was a law school in Portland called the Northwestern School of Law. This was a school that was owned and operated by the Judges and attorneys in the area. Graduation from the school provided the graduate with the right to admission to the Bar of the State of Oregon upon examination. Pre-requisite for admission was two years of college.

With my GED certificate I was two years short! However, I heard about a test administered by the Oregon State Board of Higher Education which, if passed, would provide the examinees with a two-year college equivalence. That was sufficient for admission to Northwestern Law School.

The test was scheduled for the second week of August 1964. I made application for it and proceeded to take the family on a vacation to Yellowstone Park. I was driving a Ford Fairlane station wagon with a two speed automatic transmission. I pulled a 23-foot trailer behind. Crossing into Idaho from Oregon, a loud BAM was heard. Stopping to check tires, nothing was discovered. So on we continued, stopping for the night at the Craters of the Moon National Park in Idaho.

In the morning, driving to Idaho Falls, the transmission was slipping badly. We did however get there. I had been asked by Earl Wiest, our ward bishop, to stop there and determine if a starting date could be ascertained for the new chapel to be built for the Tenth and Eleventh Wards. A building program, which the church undertook at that time, had its regional headquarters in Idaho Falls.

I put the car into a transmission shop for repairs and rented a car so the family could take a quick tour of Yellowstone. I left the trailer on a city street. That night returning from Yellowstone, the city police would not allow us to sleep in it, so we rented a motel room. In the morning, after picking up the station wagon and hooking on the trailer, we headed south to Ogden, my birthplace.

We traveled up Weber Canyon and camped out over night at a shoreline campsite. The trip that day had been a particularly bad day for relations between Pat and me. Unfortunately, the children had to bear the agony of it which they remember to this day. Again the transmission was slipping. I had to take the car to another shop for repairs in Ogden the next morning.

Some church friends of ours as well as neighbors, the Randalls, were in North Ogden visiting his family. We made contact with them, enjoying their company, while the car was repaired again. Having left the trailer up Weber Canyon, we returned that evening with a hope that the car had been fixed this time.

Early the next morning, which was Friday, we headed out for our return trip to Portland. Not far out of Ogden the transmission started slipping again. Climbing up the Blue Mountains out of LeGrand Oregon, one of the pistons blew a hole in the top of it thus allowing explosions into the crankcase. The force was so great the oil dipstick was blown out. I disconnected the spark wire and drove on down to Pendleton, where a garage mechanic told me I would have to leave the car over the weekend for repairs.

I explained I had to get back to Portland that night. I had to sit for a test at 8:00 am. The next day. He then took out the spark plug and hammered the points together. After replacing the plug he reconnected the spark plug wire. "This will let you get safely home, but you will be running on only seven cylinders," he said.

About 2:30 the next morning we pulled into our driveway. I slept little and was in downtown Portland for the 8:00 am. test. Normally going through a situation like we had the day before, I would have canceled my plans for Saturday. But in this case, I was driven by some sense of urgency to get home for that test. As it turned out later, it was the very last time the test was administered. Looking back on it, the preceding week was a stressful, disastrous time. If the "Devil "was trying to deter me, he didn't succeed!

Chapter Eleven

Some Spiritual Things

Between the marriage of 1953 and the death of John Kennedy in November of 1963, there were some significant events in my life which conditioned my mind to accept direction from a source of energy outside of myself.

Without doubt, the first event was the birth of my oldest daughter, Theresa (Teri) Lynn. As I looked at her moments after birth, my eyes watered, to see this fair "Dresden Doll," with perfectly formed little fingers and assure blue eyes. I was riding on a "high". Out of this frustrating marriage came this beautiful child. I thanked God and determined, then and there, that I would go through hell if necessary to keep my marriage intact so that this child would never be subjected to a broken marriage while she lived at home. That commitment, which I kept, also provided a cover for the other children of the marriage born after her. That included Cynthia, James, Kevin and Jennifer. Each of them has their very own special traits and personalities. I was and have always been grateful to God for them for they have made me a proud father.

Mormonism is more than a religion; it becomes literally a way of life. To be active in the church requires a dedication of one's time and energy. During the first decade after the wedding I was involved in the young people's organization called the "Mutual Improvement Association" (MIA) both in the Ward and Stake levels. Sundays were busy teaching the adult gospel doctrine class and priesthood classes.

But my problems with making a profit at building houses persisted. It caused me a great deal of distress. One Saturday night in the spring of 1958, after retiring, I spent a great deal of time in prayerful meditation about the matter.

In the morning I awoke with sun streaming through the window. The time was 5:45. I determined I could catch a little more sleep before arising for attendance at priesthood meeting. Closing my eyes, I found myself in a large palatial room.

I was seated along a wall, with several people seated to my left. Across the room were two doors. At each door stood an attendant dressed in white clothing.

From time to time, one or the other attendant would cross the room and beckon the individual seated to the extreme left to follow. No words were spoken. The individual was guided through the door of that attendant. Later, the attendant from the other door would come over and take the next individual. No individual was seen again, causing me to wonder what happened to them. Alternating from door to door, the process was repeated until it was my turn.

I was lead through the first door which quietly closed behind me. The room was in total darkness. A sudden explosion of light calmed my worst fears! I soon determined that the light did not come from a window or from artificial lighting. It emanated from a human form of intense brightness which was suspended within the room. The form was ageless. Attire consisted of the finest of white embroider garments. Hands and arms were exposed as well as neck and face. Hair was a luminous red; that is, light also emanated from the hair. I noticed no lines or wrinkles on the face of this personage. There was no evidence of sagging flesh. No effect from years of gravity with which we associate wisdom. Yet, there was a sense of supreme wisdom and knowledge present.

A feeling of peace and calm overwhelmed my soul. Here I felt the presence of the "Prince of Peace"! With a gentile smile this personage, calling me by name, asked me how he could help me. I expressed my deep concerns about my business, and a desire to do well by people in my dealings. My apparent inability to make a profit sufficient to provide extras for my family and remain solvent troubled me deeply.

Without a moment's hesitation, the personage began, "The Housing Administrator reflects his own personal opinion about the values that are placed upon the properties which you are to build. **Disregard those values**. Continue to put in place your best workmanship and materials, keeping accurate cost records.

Ask a selling price which will provide coverage for all those costs together with what you deem is enough to provide for your family and all will go well for you." Added was, "These trials and tribulations are being given you to prepare you for a future work for me."

The light was gone. Intense darkness filled the room. I had a sense of descent. In that descent, another personage met me. I could barely see the outline of the face of this personage who posed the question, "Who were you just talking to?" My response was," I was talking to the Savior".

"Savior? What Savior? There is no Savior!" was the reply. Great fear came over my soul for surely there stood the prince of darkness. Mustering great energy, I demanded departure of this personage, calling on the name of Jesus Christ! In a second I was alone again.

Just as quickly, my eyes were open with the bright sun illuminating the bedroom. I pondered the event. Surely, the advice was excellent, had I inquired of any person skilled in such things, the advice would have been the same. When Pat awoke, I related the experience to her. She wept for she believed it was a real event.

I followed that advice of disregarding FHA values for a time which meant **speculative construction only** and of course things went well. Later, however, I submitted to a fast talking real estate salesman and allowed myself to return to the construction of a few FHA valued houses on a contract basis for buyers. My prior troubles revisited me as I had again become unassertive of my own interests and was beating myself up for it. It was at this time I first felt the need to obtain more academic education.

Chapter Twelve

Two More Years of Academic Delay

Saturday morning at 8 am. I began taking the test along with about sixty others, which could, if passed, give me a two year college equivalence to allow me entrance into Northwestern School of Law. It took all day to finish.

A week or so later, the results were in and I was notified by the Oregon State Board of Higher Education that I had passed. Later I learned that only one third of those sitting for the exam passed it.

On the trip to Idaho Falls, earlier, I had learned that our Tenth Ward of the church along with the Eleventh Ward would be able to soon start construction of the new building, which would also become the Portland Stake Center. Construction was scheduled by the Regional Headquarters in Idaho Falls, to begin with ground breaking on Labor Day 1964.

Now that I had established my qualifications to enter law school, I decided to delay entrance for a year to allow me to contribute a lot of labor to the construction of the new church building.

There were many problems concerning getting the church building underway. The superintendent working for the church did not get along well with local leaders and was replaced. I had been involved with Bishop Wiest in obtaining approval from the Stake President to instigate a program of local members supervising certain crafts or trades of work on the building.

One day in the spring of 1965, I received a telephone call from the Stake Clerk requesting me to meet with the Stake President. At the appointed hour, I learned that the purpose was not to discuss the building but rather, to inform me that Bishop Earl Wiest had placed my name as a candidate for replacing a member of the Bishopric. I was somewhat stunned, yet honored, by this news.

It had been my intention to enter law school in the fall of 1965 and so informed the Stake President. It would not be possible to do both so I declined the Bishop Counselor's position.

Upon arriving home, Pat learned of the events of the evening, and went into one of her tirades. This, she said, was the first time I had the opportunity for advancement in the church, and I had turned it down! I listened to this all evening and half the night.

Going to priesthood meeting in the morning, I told Earl the predicament my decision had made in my marriage. Earl and I had been very close friends for a number of years, hunting and fishing together when times allowed. He asked me to reconsider; telling me that he wanted me to go to school, but that he and the first Counselor would cover for me.

As result of that, I told the Stake President I would set aside my plans for law school. This made Pat happy. She could then feel important as the wife of a member of the Bishopric. First, I had some problems to deal with.

It had been necessary for me to contact two members of the Stake High Council, who advise the Stake President on matters affecting the local church. My name had been presented to them and unanimously approved. However, one of the members of the Council approached the Stake President afterwards and questioned my business ethics.

The individual had been my electrical contractor on homes I had been building for eight or nine years. Due to the financial problems, which I have described before, he was a creditor, whom I had never fully paid up. It became necessary for me to attempt to make peace with this "brother".

At this period of my life, I had discontinued contracting and was employed as construction manager for John G. Clarke, Realtor, a large real estate company in Portland.

The problem was that since I was construction manager for J.G. Clarke, I did not use this individual regularly, as his bids were often too high.

During the time of my own contracting, he had the run of things, doing his work on a time and materials basis. I had trusted him as a brother in the church to be fair and honest in his dealings with me. I later learned that his bids for the same work for Clarke were considerably lower.

According to estimates I made, based upon more recent bidding, I had overpaid him some twelve thousand dollars during the time of our association. This situation never resolved itself because I refused to deepen my losses with him and he felt too "righteous" to ever forgive me. Two other individuals within the church, also subcontractors of my work, came to settlement and accord. They, of course, had not been blatantly dishonest with me.

In the spring of 1965, I was ordained a "High Priest" and set apart as a member of the Tenth Ward Bishopric of the Portland Stake of the Mormon Church.

I served in that capacity for about two years. In the summer of 1966, I told Earl that I wanted to be released so that I could attend law school. He encouraged me to start school but to stay in the Bishopric. It was decided we would not broadcast news of the decision to the Stake President. About the same time, the new ward building was completed.

One singular event happened during the spring of 1966 that had an effect upon my future life. I was at the time, building a motel addition for my relatives in Depoe Bay, Oregon. This required my staying there nights during the week from Monday to Friday.

In the Bishopric, the three members rotate responsibility, whereby one of them will be responsible to conduct all meetings on a Sunday. At this time our ward was meeting in the same building with the Seventh Ward. We had outgrown the Odd Fellows Hall we had been meeting in for several years in the Lents area of Portland.

On this particular Sunday, it was my turn to conduct meetings. I was extremely busy and somewhat stressed when I heard a statement from one of the priesthood members to the effect that the church had invented an electronic system which would help it

"Save" the United States Constitution. That news was all stir in the priesthood meeting early in the morning and discussed by many. I had too much on my mind to make further inquiries.

After that first burst of grapevine news, the subject was never heard of again. It caused me to wonder what it was all about. Some two years later, I learned more about the system. I will detail my reaction at that time later in this book.

I gave my oldest son Jimmy a new bicycle for his ninth birthday on August 1, 1966. He went with a couple of other boys up a steep hill and had an accident on the way back. He was not familiar enough with hand brakes and clamped down on the front wheel first. That caused him to take a spill which resulted in a great deal of trauma. We almost lost Jimmy that day. Bishop Wiest, a dentist, went to the hospital and wired up Jimmy's jaw. I had been out of town at the time of the accident but Pat and I were grateful for all the help and support given us that day. Within days of that accident I would be entering law school and starting a period of new adventure.

Chapter Thirteen

The Law Student

Making application for enrollment in school became another challenge since local Lewis and Clark College had acquired Northwestern Law School with the purpose in mind of obtaining accreditation with the American Bar Association. Accreditation would allow graduates to take bar exams anywhere in the country.

There was a problem however; pre-requisite education requirements had been increased from two to three years of college. I met with the new dean and pled my case. He allowed me to be enrolled as a special student. That status was allowed by the ABA for a small percentage of the student body.

My sister Jean's husband, Don, enrolled with me. This was the second time he had entered law school. The first time he did not complete for reasons I cannot remember. The second time he had to drop out as his work, as a Hearing Officer for the Oregon State Tax Commission, took him to Eastern Oregon for a duration of time that made it impossible to attend classes.

This was a new experience for me. I had not been a student in a classroom for about 21 years. All of the students, except one, were much younger. Some of them were clerking for judges of the Oregon Circuit Court in Portland. That fact alone made the situation very competitive.

Our daughter Jennifer was just a year old and Pat became very concerned about my going to school. In fact, she panicked that we would not be able to handle the financial burden. She went to work part time working two or three nights a week. The costs of her uniforms, car gas, a babysitter for Jeni, etc., when coupled with a higher tax bracket her income placed us; actually resulted in a no gain situation.

Some 36+ law subjects were studied during the four years of night law school. Classes were held Mondays, Wednesdays and

80

Fridays from six to ten pm. Summers were free of school. However, one summer, as I recall it was 1968, the class had to take a special course. This was because the instructor, a retired judge, died in his sleep while grading the term exam papers.

There were several students with whom some comradeship developed. Among these were Jim Auxier, Alex Christy and Don McCulloch. In later years, Jim and Alex did some legal work for me. Don was a schoolteacher in the Kelso-Longview area of Washington. It was with his assistance that I was able to pass the Washington State Bar exam in January of 1971. Governor Dixie Lee Ray later appointed Don a Superior Court Judge in Cowlitz County.

With work often out of Portland, it was very trying to keep the school schedule. By dedicating myself however, I missed very few classes. I had promised the Dean, who had admitted me under special status, that I would put in my best effort. Unfortunately, there was little time to study. Generally, I would have to read a case before class began. Then read the next case, while at the same time listening to the class discussion about the previous case.

After the second year, an Ivy League professor replaced The Law School Dean. This was done to bring the school into better imagery for accreditation. The school had promised the students beginning in my class (which would be the class of 1970) that the school would be fully accredited so that the students could apply for admission to any Bar in the United States.

The new Dean taught Tax Law. This was an area, which I excelled in. There were many times when mental notes were taken of tax considerations, which had an inner feeling of personal importance to me.

At this point, I want the reader to understand the continuing underlying spiritual quest to achieve a destiny which the experience on the Lincoln Elementary School grounds in 1937 had been subliminally infused in me. Going to law school was not for making money and becoming wealthy. It was not and never had been my ambition to do so. There was something deep within me that would never seek that. My concerns about

81

making a profit in construction also had nothing to do with gaining wealth. Those concerns dealt only with providing adequately for my family.

During the first term, Criminal Justice was taught. I will always remember certain established facts of law. These facts became important to me when played against my background in the Mormon Church.

The first was learning that the beginning level of criminal judicial determination was not within the court system, but rather at the office of the prosecuting attorney. This was true whether local, State or Federal. If that attorney decided not to prosecute a crime, that decision was defacto judicial. As I began to understand it, a political power base could commit unlawful acts without penalty. This would be especially true if the prosecuting attorney had a conflict of interest with that power base. One can look at the situation in Mormon Utah and understand why constitutional law is violated daily.

Another was the legal definition of insane delusion. That definition was held to be: "An incorrigible belief in an idea based upon a false premise." In the law, there is no definition of insanity other than a deviation from normal behavior within a given society. Therefore, conduct or action that would be sane within one society would not likely be for another. In that context, the situation in Yugoslavia as of this writing (May 1999), wherein ethnic cleansing has reigned, would not be insane in local custom, but would be to world thinking and acting otherwise.

My interest in the definition of insane delusion took on large proportions at the time because of my Mormon background. If a false premise was at the root of Mormon belief, then an incorrigible belief in the system, as held by Mormon people, would constitute an insane delusion. It then behooved me to seek answers to the underlying premise.

One Monday in January 1970, there was a snowstorm in Portland. I had been working on the Oregon coast and had to drive to Portland to school. It was the first of the new term. I was late getting to class. Another student was also late, as we had to park some distance away from the campus and hike in. We took seats in the rear of the room, as was always my custom.

The first class was Evidence. It was to be taught by an R. Jones. I knew nothing of this instructor. Arriving a few minutes late, this instructor ordered my companion and me to the front of the class. My companion went, I remained seated. Again, this instructor ordered me to the front. I told him I would prefer to stay seated where I was. "You get up here," he stated. I made a split-second decision about the future of my law education. I said to him, "You can take your class and go to hell." As I did so, I got up and began walking out of the class.

He shouted at me, "What is your name?" I responded. He than began to back down explaining to me that he wanted some students at the front to demonstrate an incident of evidence. I told him that was different; if that were his intent, I would comply. However, I told him I was a little too old to be disciplined for being late. The class at the time was all frozen in place at this event. I later learned that I had challenged Judge Robert Jones of the Oregon Circuit Court. Many of the class members came to me after class and said, "Boy is he ever going to do you in on grades."

He skillfully turned the confrontation into an evidence question for the class by asking several of them to relate what they had witnessed. There were a number of discrepancies.

Judge Robert Jones had a reputation of calling down attorneys in his courtroom, if they were late, ill prepared, or not adequately attired. Since some of the class members were clerking for other judges in the same court, rumors flew around court the next day that a third year law student had called down "Little Caesar".

At the end of the school year, Judge Jones came to me and related what he thought the students would think of his actions regarding me. He said that they all felt he would do me in on final grades. He did not, as I received a good grade from him. He did tell me he respected me for standing up to him. Judge Jones later became a United States District Court Judge.

During the first year of law school, I remained a member of the Tenth Ward Bishopric. I missed meetings of the bishopric that were held during the week. Earl and Herb were supposed to keep me informed of events but failed to do so, probably because of the pressures my absence placed on them.

One Sunday morning it was my turn to conduct meetings and to be responsible for the building even staying late to make sure it was locked up after everyone had left. It also happened to be annual ward conference when the Stake Presidency would be there.

As I walked up the aisle to the podium for early morning priesthood meeting, I received first word of my having been selected by the bishopric in their mid week meeting without me, that I was to be the speaker for the ward in that meeting. Panic struck, as I had no preparation whatever and this was to be done in just a few minutes!

I went straight for the Bishop's office, where I saw a Bible on the desk. As I walked back towards the podium, I allowed the book to fall open. It opened at John 21: verses 15-17, where Christ thrice asked Peter if he loved him.

When I stood up to conduct the priesthood meeting, I placed the open Bible on the podium. As the time came to give my talk (sermon), I began by stating my concerns about the Home Teaching Program of the church. No sooner did I do so than I became aware of eyes staring at me from the Stake President, Thomas Y. Emmett, with whom I had had a prior confrontation over the subject. I turned to look at him and sure enough, he had the look of disgust on his face.

Nevertheless, I went on and delivered an extemporaneous talk on the subject, using the biblical passage lying before me as the foundation. After the meeting was over, Reed Madsen of the Stake Presidency came to me and said he couldn't believe my talk was extemporaneous, as it was the finest sermon he had ever heard. I was responsible in the ward for the Home Teaching program. Two elders who had not been doing their teaching came to me separately and stated they had never before realized the purpose of the program, and then and there committed themselves to do the work.

Later, I told Earl that I had stumbled into a pit of confrontation with the Stake President again (A similar situation had occurred during a previous Stake Conference.). I also told him that I had provided him with a topic for his speech that evening and that it would be revisited. Earl told me that lightening does not strike twice in the same place and to not worry.

That evening, when the time came for The Stake President's speech, surely enough the topic was revisited. Beginning with, "This morning in the priesthood meeting, Brother Wallace..." Approximately 40 minutes was utilized. At conclusion, he turned to me and said," Brother Wallace, I hope this will finally make you understand the importance of the Home Teaching program."

I was stunned by his conduct! In the morning, there were less than a hundred men to whom I delivered my speech. In the evening, there were well over four hundred members most of whom did not hear what I had to say in the morning. The Stake President, before members of the ward I served, was publicly dressing me down. It was an unconscionable thing for him to do.

Later that evening, I ran into him at the door to the Bishops office. He being somewhat shorter than I looked up and said to me, "Brother Wallace, I hope you don't mind my having quoted you." I told him that his position allowed him to do what he felt best but that the issue was not resolved. I told him I agreed with every thing he had said but that he missed my point altogether. The problem was not the honor to be given the title of "teacher". It was in the naming of the program. He responded by saying the program was revelation from God and that was that! I retorted, "Just like Ward Teaching and Block Teaching before it?" Both of those programs were failures.

At home, Pat, who had been present at the meeting said, "Well, President Emmett sure put you in your place!" This event caused me a great deal of personal distress. My intention and purpose was to do what my intelligence told me was right. I had again been honest with myself and gotten into seeming trouble over it. I had nonetheless again demonstrated my strength to challenge authority, when I felt it was needed. This kind of action on my part would later cause me to be excommunicated from the church for insubordination.

For the moment, my thoughts were introspective. Why did Emmett do such a thing to me? I lay awake at night thinking on it. Why? Why? Why?

In the arena of the mind where answers come to solve dilemma, the words came, "Satan is doing every thing in his power to thwart you." To that I answered, <u>again only in</u> <u>thought</u>, "I have heard that all my life! (Referring to my Patriarchal Blessing) Why?" Then came words, "David O. McKay is lingering while you prepare yourself."

Pondering on that thought, I arose out of bed and went to the living room, where I knelt at the couch and prayed to God for Satan to leave. It, the thought of succeeding McKay, was totally opposite instruction I had received all my life. One did not seek office! Only Satan could cause one to seek exaltation in this world! (A strange notion in view of the fact that Mormonism trains one to seek Godhood!)

Pat, noticing my absence from the bed, came to the living room and asked what the matter was. I told her what had happened and she said, "Wow, you are getting out of line!"

I put this experience aside, but have to admit that my future conduct within the church had this backdrop, which would gain a larger scenario over the next few years. Shortly after that experience, I resigned from the bishopric to concentrate on law school.

In the fall of 1969, a former deputy of the Multnomah County District Attorney's office, a Billy Williamson became a full time faculty member of Northwestern School of law. The hiring of full time faculty was another requisite for accreditation of the school. He taught administrative law. At the beginning of the term he had each of the students draw out of a hat a topic which would have to be dealt with by writing a legal brief on the subject.

Tenth Ward Bishopric Portland Stake 1965-1967 Herb Hill 1st Counselor, Bishop Earl Wiest, Author 2nd Counselor in the Bishop's Office of new ward chapel

My subject was THE EFFECTIVENESS OF THE EQUAL OPPORTUNITY COMMISSION [EOC] IN THE HIRING OF MINORITIES IN THE CONSTRUCTION INDUSTRY.

Well, I considered that a breeze! Certainly, my experience in construction would make it easy. So as usual, being strapped for time, I decided to put off research until the Christmas Holidays.

When that time came, I scheduled a meeting with the EOC officer for the Associated General Contractors Association (AGC). The Gentleman I met with painted a beautiful picture of compliance on the part of the association.

I next went to Urban League. The spokesperson there was a very good communicator of the English language. He painted an entirely different picture. I had now opened a Pandora's Box and knew I could not write the paper during the Christmas break.

At that particular time in history, University athletic teams around the country were boycotting Brigham Young University (BYU) teams over the issue of the Mormon Church, which owned BYU. They did not allow black men to be ordained priests in the church.

While with that gentleman at Urban League, I posed a question to him. I asked him why that was being done. With some disgust toward me showing on his face, he answered, "Because that denial is a vestige of discrimination. We in the black community will challenge any and all such vestiges of discrimination!"

I made an appointment with Billy Williamson to discuss my dilemma. I requested that he allow me to turn in the paper the next term, as I needed the time to travel to San Francisco, regional headquarters of the EEOC, to make a full study.

His response was that he didn't think the other members of the faculty would go along with that or for that matter didn't then know what value, if any, he would give the legal briefs to the term grades.

I was a little surprised to hear what next came out of his mouth. "You are a Mormon are you not?" I answered in the affirmative. He asked, "As a substitution, will you consider writing a legal brief for the first law review publication the school is planning for next summer?" Then he suggested I write a brief on the subject of whether or not the Mormon Church was violating the civil rights of black men by denying them priesthood! I told him I would think on it.

Wow! Oh boy! That put me in a difficult situation! My sentiments were always in conflict with the official church stance. Since the decision on my part was of urgency, for the school term was about to end, and exams coming up, I had to make the issue a part of my daily thought processes.

Saturday night January 17, 1970 found me sitting up in bed studying for term exams. After several hours of study into the early hours of the 18th, I laid my materials aside, shut off the bedside lamp and engaged in prayerful meditation on the subject of the law review article.

In the previous decade, David O. McKay had dedicated the Mormon Temple in Oakland California. A black reporter from the local newspaper asked him when the Mormon Church would give priesthood to black men.

"Not in my lifetime young man, nor yours," was the reply. This event had been chronicled in the church monthly magazine the ENSIGN at the time of the dedication of the temple.

As I had always to this time considered McKay a prophet of God; my dilemma was in confronting him over the issue. While I deeply knew the policy was neither Of God nor even Christian, I asked in my prayer, "How can I write this article while he is alive?"

The next morning I took the children to Sunday school and went back home to study more for the exams. When I drove up to the rear door of the ward house, and waited for the children, my second daughter Cynthia, then about 14, was the first to appear at the car.

"Did you hear what happened to President McKay last night," was her urgent question. I told her I had not, to which she responded; "He died!"

Oh God! I felt the weight of his death on my shoulders. My prayer and his death were only moments apart, when considering the one-hour time difference. I was now free to write the article. However, the event of the spring of 1967 was brought to the front of my mind. What was meant by the words, "David O. McKay is lingering while you prepare yourself"?

The next morning I called Don Wood, a former president of the Northwestern States Mission of the church, who lived in our ward and was a research biochemist working for Providence Hospital in Portland. I arranged a luncheon date with him.

Don had been a friend and confidant for several years. A couple of years earlier, I had met with him to consider the possible apostasy that I might be going through at the time. He assured me I was not and that God had some purpose in my going to law school. He had said, "what ever you need to do, I will support you."

So, here at the luncheon table, several hours were consumed with my unloading on him a number of spiritual events of my life, including the event of 1967. Did God want me to succeed McKay? He said he would contact the "Brethren", meaning the Apostles of the church, about the matter.

During the meeting, the subject of black priesthood arose. He asked me what my position was. I responded, "The same as Christ's." "What is that," he asked. At that moment a voice came out of my mouth that was *not my own*. Don was stunned by the sound of that voice, as was I. The words uttered were, "Call not unclean that which I have cleansed!" After recovery, I said any person baptized into the church was cleansed by the blood of Christ and worthy of receiving all rights and blessings of God, regardless of color or ethnic background.

Don's head had involuntarily thrust backward for a moment at the sound of the voice. We then continued our conversation. Before we parted, however, he remarked that he did not agree with me on the black priesthood issue.

Don later said he had called a friend on the Mormon council and was told the Apostles had a lot on their mind just then. My contacting Don was timely to determine an answer to a dilemma confronting me. Yet it would be many years before an answer came and I had to find it myself.

Joseph Fielding Smith, as the senior member of the quorum, was installed as the next church president. Shortly after, I told my two oldest daughters that if my precognition was correct, Smith would not live more than thirty months and would die sitting in a chair. It turned out to be true.

The traumatic experience of having to confront the issue of writing a law review article about the Mormon Church and black priesthood as it turned out was moot. The legal briefs were not weighed and I was excused for failure to turn one in. I was not asked again about the issue of black priesthood. However, I had confronted it and was given a clear signal to again deal with it when it was timely for me.

Some 108 students had registered for the class of 1970. Attrition took its toll; there were 35 who graduated. My ranking was 34th. I have always said that I graduated among the top 1/3rd of the starting class. That sounds more impressive!

Therefore, in June 1970 I was among those who received a Juris Doctor degree. (J.D) Accreditation had been secured allowing students to sit for bar exams anywhere in the U.S. Four years of exacting energy were over. The future however would hold a time of more conditioning of my character; a time of commitment and posture to act in support of my beliefs.

PORTLAND STAKE PRESIDENCY

Grant K. Remington   Thomas Y. Emmett   Reed R. Madsen
1st Counselor   President   2nd Counselor

Portland Stake Presidency at time Author was a member of the Tenth
Ward Bishopric. Author had two clashes with Thomas Emmett over
Home Teaching Program. Reed Madsen is remembered by the Author
as a very kind individual

Chapter Fourteen

The Graduate

After graduation, the next challenge would be passing a bar exam. Early in 1970, I had moved my family from Portland to Woodland, Washington. Woodland was a small logging community on the Lewis River. Interstate 5 bisected the community. I had run across a very nice home that had settlement problems on its hillside setting. Believing I could resolve those problems, I accepted title subject to the mortgage since I did not want liability if my efforts to save the house proved futile. We moved into it shortly after the winter term exams had been completed. I rented out the house in Portland.

Looking back on that situation, my oldest daughter Teri had been setting the curve at David Douglas High School in Portland for two years. She found the small high school in Woodland to offer little challenge. She did share in all of the honors along with the son of the district superintendent. It became embarrassing at graduation to have to repeatedly stand as her parent when the honors were announced. Yet, I was proud of her for her achievements. I had great expectations of her.

The well casing of the house on the hill had been sheared or bent by the sliding of the hill. Temporary water connection was made with a neighbor, but he demanded I repair the well as soon as school was out.

I had made application to sit for the Oregon bar exam that summer. To prepare for it, I enrolled in a bar review course at Willamette University in Salem, Oregon.

Therefore, I spent weekends at home attempting to restore the well, and weekdays at Willamette staying with my sister Jean at night Monday through Thursday. This went on for about six weeks.

I ran into all kinds of problems with the well. The manner of my operation was to first set a 3-foot high concrete well ring over the well casing. I positioned the ring so that the well casing was on the downhill wall of the concrete ring. Then, digging out dirt from the inside bottom of the ring, it would gradually settle. As it did, I would add another ring on top. In this manner, I dug down about twenty feet before discovering the well casing was bent on about a 45degree angle toward the uphill side of the concrete ring. In time, I found it to have traveled outside of the concrete ring. I had to break out the uphill side of the ring to locate the original well casing below. It was discovered to be about twelve inches on the outside.

It became necessary for removal, to use a cutting torch to severe the six inch well casing from the bent and useless casing above it. The first effort at lighting the torch and cutting was quickly halted due to the profuse smoke which emitted from the operation. I then took a long piece of 2" plastic pipe and placed it down inside the concrete rings. I had connected the pipe to a vacuum blower on the ground. This worked quite well and kept the working area free of noxious fumes.

My older kids had been attendants at the top of the well cranking up the buckets of dirt on a windless. When they witnessed all the smoke billowing up, they began to scream about my safety. However, in my arena it was quite clear.

I was able to make a repair to the well and get it back into operation. However, the hill later slid more and took it out again about two years later. I relate this story to show how I allowed the well problem to interfere with my studying for the Oregon Bar exam in July. I did not pass that exam. Since Oregon only gave the bar exam once a year, and I now lived in Washington, I looked to Washington State to take the January 1971 exam.

My friend Don McCullough had successfully taken the Washington exam in July. He loaned his bar review materials to me so I could bone up for the exam in January. As I recall, the exam took the better part of three days. This time I passed it!

This was a time of deep introspection for me! Always in the back of my head was the repressed memory of the incident on the Lincoln Grade School playground back on May 8th 1937. I had remembered little bits of it but not the entire experience. Somehow, I knew it portended a part of my future life.

Then there was the experience in 1967 where a voice within my head made the statement about the lingering of David O. McKay. That, coupled with the law school experience of having to make a decision about writing a law review article on Black priesthood denial in the Mormon Church, and the timeliness of the death of McKay, triggered me to seek answers as to whether God intended I should become an instrument in His hand.

There were, of course, other items such as the Bee lapel pin used for political spying by elders of the church*. A vision of a World Peace monument at Jerusalem which I later made an oil painting of: The dream of 1957 wherein I was advised my experiences were training for a future work for God, etc.

*[In the spring of 1968, Earl Wiest and I were fishing for salmon on the Columbia River As we would spend the day mostly talking, I had remembrance of the 1966 gossip flurry at priesthood meeting. I asked him what that was all about He said that an elder of the church living in our ward had special general church duties as a part of the church security (I had often wondered why Farley Sawyer*** could never be called to fill a job within the ward}. Attending a special meeting of church security at the spring conference in Salt Lake City. Entering the meeting late, he had missed out on a preliminary commitment to blood oath secrecy about what was to be discussed. It appeared the church had developed secret spy technology by which "elders" of the church wearing a lapel pin could eavesdrop on any meeting anywhere and have the conversation recorded in Salt Lake City. I asked Earl what the pin would look like to which he replied in the form of a bee. Very fitting for the Beehive State of Deseret. (Utah). I asked for what purpose. The reply. "To save the Constitution", an old ambition of the church. My response was that it was the most diabolical scheme I had ever heard of and that if I ever heard more about it by word of mouth or by revelation, I would expose it to the world. With fear in his eyes and voice, Earl said," **you wouldn't**". I said yes and at that moment I had a flash vision of my doing that in the Coliseum Travelodge so I told Earl I would do it and where. I will later detail more about that technology. Earl went on to say that after word got back to the Stake President that Farley was gagged and nothing more was said.]*

*** Name Changed

This is a facsimile of the lapel pin in 3 sizes

It became very important for me now at the age of 41 to make a determination if those entire spiritual experiences which I had had, held some real purpose in my future life. Perhaps even more important to me was discovery of the truth. Only knowing the truth would set me free. My lifetime in Mormonism had produced all of those experiences. Either they were true or they were false. If they were false then likely Mormonism was false also.

This is an area of the spiritual nature of man which has produced many of the world's religions. You can read of such things happening to others in different ages but when they happen to you it is different. Was I losing my own sanity? How could I practice law in a very pragmatic world while at the same time holding to what could only be regarded as revelation from God? My first priority now was to find out!

Chapter Fifteen

Questions of Sanity

Wallace Teuscher, was a dentist whom I had known for a number of years. I first met him when he was a student at The University of Oregon Dental School in Portland, Oregon back in the fifties. A Mormon, he had been "called" to be president of the North Columbia River Stake of the church. That Stake was centered in Vancouver, Washington.

Living in Woodland, Washington at this time; attending the Woodland Ward, a part of the North Columbia River Stake, and being a High Priest of the church, I had frequent contact with him.

Within a very short time after passing the Bar, I made an appointment with Wally. We met at his home in his study. I related to him all of the spiritual events that had transpired in my life which caused me to think God had a special mission for me. The only item not related was the 8th birthday event which I could not remember much of anyhow.

When I finished, he was eager that we take a plane to Salt Lake City and present this information to the "Brethren". I cautioned him to think on this for a while. Since he was to attend the Woodland Ward the next Sunday, he said he would confer with me about it then.

Next Sunday, he took me aside and told me that after reflecting on the matter he felt I should seek the counsel of a psychiatrist, and that I spend a year of introspection about my life to see why these things had happened to me.

I agreed to do that. Belonging to the Kaiser Health Plan, I made an appointment with a Dr. Richard Gregory at the Portland clinic.

A week or two later, Wally asked me if I was following his advice. I replied I was and that I was having sessions with a psychiatrist.

He seemed alarmed about that and excitedly asked if the Dr. was a Christian! His question puzzled me, and I asked why would that make any difference? If I was nuts, I was nuts, Christian or not! It was a medical question! A questioning shrug was his only response. Wally and I did not talk about this again for a year.

Therefore, for the next twelve weeks or so I had 30-minute interviews with Dr. Gregory. At conclusion, he stated there was no reason for me to continue coming. He stated that I had no delusional problems. I knew who I was and what my limitations were. He suggested the problem was solely theological and I would have to work it out myself. He did suggest that I felt destined to challenge authority, be it in private organizations, associations or religion.

At the conclusion of sessions with him, I commenced building a law office in Woodland Washington.

I took out a commercial loan which funded the building (Earl Wiest had participated). I started it in September 1971 and finished it in May 1972, building it entirely by myself. When completed, or even before, I began a part time practice of law. Martha Saunders***, a member of the church, and our new neighbor on the hill, agreed to be my legal secretary. She had been doing that In Idaho. She and her husband Paine***moved to Woodland where he was employed as vice president of a Bank. They had two children and would be involved in my life for the next two years or so.

*[*** Names have been changed.]*

Shortly after starting construction of the law office, it was necessary for me to transport my Daughter Teri to Brigham Young University. We traveled to Provo, Utah in a Datsun pickup. It had a camper shell and we could carry all of her belongings in it. After getting Teri settled into her campus dorm, I left Provo and started back toward Salt Lake City.

Barely two miles away, a piston rod came loose in the engine. I crept up the old Draper highway to SLC. This was on a Saturday and nothing could be done about the engine until Monday. I called my old missionary companion, Grant Hardy from a motel room. He invited me to Sunday dinner. The next morning would begin a week of most exciting adventure.

Grant was Chairman of the General Church Family Home Evening Committee. That group planned the manual which would each year guide church families in conducting their Monday evenings at home together. This was a part of the co-ordinated programs the church had established a few years earlier.

A woman member of that committee sat in the front passenger seat when Grant arrived at my motel shortly after noon. I sat in the back seat and was introduced to her. She was very upset as I could tell from her discussion with Grant. Seeing I was embarrassed by the situation, Grant explained to me that this sister had written her lessons for inclusion in the next (1972) family Home Evening Manual. The General Authority (member of the Council of the Twelve) who oversaw the activities of that committee had rejected the content of the sister's material as saying it would put out a wrong message to church members.

Inquiring further, I learned the lesson had clearly shown that family came first and church second. In illustrating her point, this sister told a story about a woman who had devoted her life to the church to the exclusion of her own family. When a son became entangled in a wayward fashion, this mother belatedly attempted to show real concern for this son. He rejected her, saying that she had never been concerned about him before as she always had let her "church duties" keep her from being close.

The author wanted to point out that before one can have time to engage in church activities, one must first be responsible for family. I agreed with her to which she said," I like you!" Grant then said that was the one thing he liked about me, that is, I always said it like it was.

That afternoon after a very sumptuous meal prepared by Grant's wife Janal, Grant and I sat in the back yard discussing items about the church. We first discussed the razing of the old Stake Tabernacle at Coalville, Utah.

This had been the subject of protest by those who wanted it preserved as an historic site. The conflict was suppressed by a statement from Harold B. Lee, then President of the Council of the Twelve, that the church would not dismantle it until after a complete study had been made. That night, crews with wrecking equipment went in and leveled it!

This deception and dishonesty on the part of church officials was discussed. Later Grant was to make the statement to me that Harold B. Lee "wouldn't lie" to the world, but took a deep breath when I brought up the dishonesty about Coalville. Grant, a few years later wanted to know what I then thought of Harold B. Lee. I will detail that response later in this writing.

I took this opportunity to tell Grant about the spiritual experiences I had had and where they seemed to be leading me. I explained to him that I would challenge the church leaders if that became necessary. With a pain on his face he said, "They'll burn you!"

On Monday morning I took the Datsun pickup to a repair shop. Later I learned they would have to replace a rod and do some other work to the engine. It would take several days. I took this opportunity to look up my old boss, Julian Cannon, in the church building department.

Julian and Paul Woodruff had both gone to work for the church as soon as they graduated from college with engineering degrees. That was in the 30's and now both of them had turned 65. The church personnel department had come out with a new rule retiring everyone when they reached 65. Therefore, both Paul and Julian were on the retirement list.

Neither of them had social security and the church did not provide retirement for them. Julian had a daughter still in college and his future looked bleak, as he would have to keep on working to survive. Paul had a similar problem and both of them expressed to me their deep displeasure at the retirement policy. Julian said that it would not be so bad if everyone, including the Apostles, were forced into retirement. But, as it was, it was very unfair and discriminatory.

However, Julian had a little reprieve. He was in charge of the construction of the Church office tower at 50 East North Temple that had been many years in the building. Because of that, his retirement was deferred until construction was completed. Well, almost...

I asked Julian how tall the tower was. He responded," inside or outside?" To that I said, "What do you mean?" His reply was that the building was 30 stories tall but would have a superstructure built on top. I asked what would that be for. He said he did not know.

I proceeded to ask him what all the stories would be used for. He then told me that the first 27 would house offices for auxiliaries of the church. What would the other 3 stories be used for? "I don't know, since I have no interior finishing plans! I will be retired before that area is completed", he added." To my question, "Why, what for?" he responded, "Beats the hell out of me. But this I can say, they are building the place like a fort!"

The thought of the surveillance lapel pin, the BEE came across my mind, Earl had told me in the spring of 1968, that the spy system would be put into operation soon after the "Tower" was completed. Here we were in September of 1971 with about a year of construction left on the tower, after which, Julian Cannon would be retired and the technology for the spy system installed in the top 3 floors.

I took leave of Julian and Paul and never saw them again. As I write, (1999) they both would be 92 years of age if still alive.

As soon as the truck was repaired, I returned to Woodland. Pat had undergone a hysterectomy just a week before my taking Teri to BYU. During the time of her recuperation, we got along fine but the strife reappeared when she became well.

I worked on the law office during the winter of 1971-72 and had it ready for use in the spring.

One Sunday in early 1972 Wally Teuscher visited the Woodland Ward. He wanted to talk to me. Seated in a classroom, he said to me that it was good to see I had forgotten all about the dilemma I had approached him with a year earlier. I told him in very strong terms that it was not forgotten and that it continued to deeply trouble me. He said he would write a letter of introduction to Spencer W. Kimball for me, and that I should pursue the matter through that channel.

No sooner was my office completed and occupied when I dictated a letter to Spencer W. Kimball, now President of the Council of the Twelve. Attached to my letter was the letter of introduction written by Wally.

In a week or so, I received a reply from him stating that he was recovering from open-heart surgery and he would refer the matter to another apostle, LeGrand Richards. Richards had been the Presiding Bishop of the church for whom I worked in 1951. He had also officiated at Pat's and my marriage in the Salt Lake Temple in January 1953, so I felt comfortable with that arrangement. I wrote to Richards and he responded.

However, each time he did so, he would change the subject matter, which required that I speak to the new subject before returning to the overshadowing dilemma.

During this exchange, Joseph Fielding Smith, then president of the Mormon Church visited his daughter and while sitting in a chair in her kitchen the evening of July 3, 1972 fell over dead. This was 21 days short of the 30 months I had told my daughters, Teri and Cynthia; he would not live to if I were correct in the conclusions which my spiritual experiences [precognition] caused me to reach.

Again, I was somewhat traumatized by the event and knew not what was to follow. My concerns, as stated in the letters to Richards, were either ignored or not discussed with the quorum by Richards when they sustained Harold B. Lee as the new president of the church.

I asked Richards if he had brought the subject up with the Twelve and he responded by saying that he did not since they would think him foolish to have done so.

Because of that, I decided to write a cover letter to each member of the Twelve with copies of the exchange of correspondence between Richards and myself. I added to that a statement with signature lines for each of the Twelve to sign their concurrence with Richards with a command that I cease and desist from all further efforts in that direction with the added proviso that if they were wrong, they would take upon themselves the sin if any there be for my willful disobedience to God.

After all the materials were in sealed envelopes, I took several days for more introspection.

A dream occurred. Pat and I were driving down a long straight road through a desert. A rear tire blew out and I had to put on the spare. Being concerned about no longer having a spare, I wanted to buy one. However, there were no stations on this desert. Suddenly, a way station appeared. I pulled into it and going inside asked the attendant, dressed in white, if he had any tires for sale. He pointed to the back room.

I went there and saw 2 tires hanging on a post. One was square with a round center for mounting. It had a very deep tread, as I could put my hand into it down to the knuckles. But it was square!

The other tire was round like an ordinary tire yet it was made out of a semi-transparent material. It had no tread and appeared quite smooth. It also seemed to be as thin as a sheet of paper.

Soon the attendant came into the room and asked me if I had made my selection. I told him this was a joke. I asked him where the real tires were. He told me that was all he had. Oh yes, he had different sizes but these were the only types he had.

Then I went into an argument about the tires. The square one would be bumpy and cause all kinds of friction. It would wear thin in a hurry. "That is why it has such a deep tread, "was the answer. "But it will get you to your journey's end," he added. "In time?" I asked. The answer was, "No"

The transparent one was next. I asked what kind of material it was made out. The reply was that it was made of the most durable material discovered by man. I asked him which one he would choose if the choice were his. "The transparent one", was his response. Again I said, "what is it made of, some magic plastic?" He looked me square in the eyes and said, "Well, let's call it faith!"

I fully understood the import and requested that he replace all the tires on my vehicle with it. Seeing the transparent tires being taken out of the station to be placed on the car, Pat became ballistic. I tried to assure her that all would be well and told her we would get to our journey's end on those tires. "That is one journey I am not going on with you," was her answer, as she got out of the car.

The next day was Wednesday and Earl and I went on a fishing trip after work. We drove to the Oregon coast and slept in bags in his station wagon. I told him about the dream. That I knew I should send the material to the "Brethren" and that it was the beginning of the end for Pat and me.

The next day, all of the materials were sent out by certified mail, return receipt requested. In about ten days, those receipts started coming back to me indicating eleven of the Twelve had received a copy.

I heard from Spencer Kimball. I had not sent him anything respecting his earlier mentioning of recovering from surgery. In his letter to me, he stated that he did not think any of the Twelve would respond, but that he felt if what I had had was a revelation from God, I should merely lock it up in my heart and never tell anyone. He went on to say that when the angel told Mary she would give birth to the Son of God, she locked it up in her heart. Had she told anyone, Kimball reasoned, she would not have lived to give birth to the Savior. Additionally, he said he would appreciate a little note from me assuring him I would follow his counsel and that I would be most discreet in the questions I asked and the answers I gave in (church) class work. So much for the traditional methods of obtaining answers for my dilemma! I had chosen faith and those would be the tires I would ride on for this journey.

THE CHURCH OF JESUS CHRIST OF LATTER-DAY SAINTS
THE COUNCIL OF THE TWELVE
47 E. SOUTH TEMPLE STREET
SALT LAKE CITY, UTAH 84111

August 9, 1972

Mr. Douglas A. Wallace
566 Goerig - P. O. Box Q
Woodland, Washington 98674

Dear Brother Wallace:

I have taken the time to read the material you have sent to the Brethren. I doubt if any others will answer your letter, but I thought I would send a note to you.

If I were you, Brother Wallace, I would close the door on the past and begin immediately now to live all the commandments of the Lord and follow the Brethren, your bishop, your stake president, your quorum leaders, and have your night and morning prayers, your home evenings and do everything according to the Church program.

You will remember that when Mary received a special message from the angel that she was to be the mother of the Son of God, the scripture says, "And she treasured it in her heart." I think if she had broadcasted this information that she would not have lived to give birth to the Lord Jesus Christ. Therefore, I think that if you should have wl you felt was a revelation or a vision, merely lock it up in your own he and never tell it to anybody.

It would please me if you would drop me a little note advising that you were going to follow this counsel and even that you would be most discreet in the questions you should ask or answer in classwork.

May the Lord bless you.

Faithfully yours,

Spencer W. Kimball
President

SWK/jl

106

Chapter sixteen

The Marriage Ends

My first efforts as an attorney concerned the citizens of Woodland. The community was divided not only by the Lewis River but also by the haves and have-nots. An attorney with some years of tenure in the community seemed to enjoy the art of toying with the people. He was acting as the city attorney in addition to his private practice. In that capacity, he appeared to team up with the police chief and the local magistrate, a former local motel owner, of the municipal court.

A lot of horror stories were related across my desk. I organized Citizens for Woodland, a non profit political action group, and filed lawsuits seeking to remedy the polarity and injustice existing there. Officials of the community were named defendants.

After filing the lawsuits, I took my family to Disneyland and dropped Teri off at BYU for her second year. Upon returning to Woodland, I discovered that unknown individuals had smashed out plate glass windows of my office. I could only surmise who was responsible.

In addition, Martha announced that she was quitting and would not return after her and Paine's vacation trip to Idaho. Martha had become a friend of the legal secretary of the other attorney. This other secretary related to Martha that her boss boasted he was going to sue me and subpoena Martha as a witness against me.

That idea terrorized Martha and she chose to quit work rather than allow him to probe into confidential matters in my office. I told her that this could not be done as it violated law. Later, she said she had asked her uncle, for whom she had worked in Idaho, about it and he told her the same thing. Nevertheless, Martha did not return to work, instead, she accepted a job in Vancouver at a larger law firm where she could learn word processing. It became necessary for me to try out several secretaries over the next few months. The paper work showed it!

During that time, a couple from the Woodland Ward came to me requesting a friendly divorce. I was shocked by the request as I knew them and never guessed there was a problem. Later I realized that my own marriage appeared equally happy to other church members.

Because of the lawsuits I filed on behalf of Citizens for Woodland, some significant changes were made in the local law enforcement scene. I had attempted to get the Cowlitz County Sheriff to patrol Woodland so the city police could be eliminated. I had visited the sheriff in his office in Kelso. He seemed eager to add Woodland to his jurisdiction. However, when he appeared at the city council meeting set to discuss the item, he turned totally negative.

The next morning, in the county court house, I asked him why. He said that the other attorney had stopped in his office that afternoon and told him the council had decided they would not vote for the sheriff taking over patrol. He told me he did not want egg in his face so decided to be negative and refuse the request.

Shortly afterwards, I confronted the other attorney in the hall outside of the clerk's office. We had a loud discussion about the impropriety of his conduct. I am surprised the sheriff did not arrest the both of us for disturbing the peace!

The Woodland police chief resigned. The municipal court was taken over by the District Court judge from Kelso. The other attorney, as chairman of the Clark County Democratic Committee, (he lived in Clark not Cowlitz county) appointed himself to fill the vacancy in the office of Prosecuting Attorney for the county. All in all, the town was cleared of what had appeared to many people, as a conspiracy in law enforcement.

Martha had been quite disturbed at my having taken on the city government. To be successful financially, attorneys do not do that! However, since my becoming an attorney had to do with the future issue of challenging church authority, it was an exercise in

108

true grit for me. One could say I cut my legal teeth by taking on city hall.

My dilemma with the church continued to haunt me. I made an appointment with Dr. Gregory where I explained to him the current situation and my intention to challenge the church leadership. He gulped at the thought. Doing so would set a precedent in which members of associations would be able to challenge the status quo, altering long-standing traditions. He said he thought I ought to get a second opinion and referred me to a Dr. Paltrow.

Dr. Paltrow's modus operandi was group therapy. I am not sure if any of the group fully understood why they were there. I went several times to this once a week group. The last time, Paltrow wanted me to open and be the evening subject for discussion. A fellow in the group made the comment that all this was B.S. that Mormons were no different than any other religion. I countered by saying,"Oh yes they are!" "In what way", he said. "Well let us put it this way." I responded, "Mormons believe God is a super-star stud!".

Paltrow, himself of the Jewish faith, doubled up with laughter. Gaining composure, he stated that if the root of the problem were my marriage he would deal with it as a surgeon. I left the group telling him I would deal with the problem myself. I never went back.

At home that evening, for the first time in 20 years, I began a non-stop discourse to Pat about our marriage and the number of times she had totally disappointed me. I circled through the dining room; living room; front hall and kitchen, occasionally stopping to get a carrot or stick of celery from the refrigerator which I chewed on as I laid bare my feelings about our relationship. Pat was quite taken back that I had such pent-up frustrations and could express them so firmly but without anger. For a while, things were better between us.

One afternoon in the fall of 1972, I was conferring with clients in my office. My secretary had left at 5:00 pm. A knock sounded on the office door. At the door I discovered Martha. She said she wanted to talk to me about coming back to work. Since I had clients waiting, I suggested we meet later that evening at the office and talk about it.

At the appointed hour we met and discussed the situation. It had been a pleasant surprise to see her earlier but was shocked to experience I had very warm feelings about her. This I deemed to be inappropriate. I suggested that she continue working where she was learning computer word processing.

The next day Pat asked me if Martha was coming back and I said," No". When she asked me why I told her I discovered I had warm feelings about her. I shouldn't have them and it was best for her not to work for me. Telling Pat that was a mistake of course but then I have been known to be brutally honest! The next day Saturday, I worked at the office. In the afternoon, I received a frantic telephone call from my daughter; Cynthia, "Dad you have to come home mother has gone berserk!"

I rushed towards home. Pat was driving the Oldsmobile station wagon directly at me forcing me to run off the shoulder. At the last minute she swerved and continued on. I went to the house to find the children cowering in the basement. There was blood on the walls of the house. My garments (secret Mormon underwear) had all of the crotches chopped out with a butcher knife. They were strewn around the floor. My suits and other clothes had been thrown out on the wet backyard lawn.

Somewhere during that tirade, Pat had driven up the hill to Martha's house. Seeing her young son in the yard, Pat opened the car window and made some inappropriate statement. The son went to his father and asked what a slut was. To the question why do you want to know, the boy answered, "That's what sister Wallace said mother was"

When Pat came home, I told her she was completely out of line. There was no impropriety with Martha and she owed Martha and Paine an apology. Shortly after that, Earl and I went on a sports outing. Afterward, driving up the common driveway we shared with Paine and Martha, I told Earl about the event and that someday I may be excommunicated from the church for insubordination but never for adultery!

110

It wasn't long before the situation became so difficult with Pat that I moved to a motel. However, when the holiday season came on, I felt lonely without the kids and moved back. The holidays were very strained. Nothing had been resolved by my returning home. Even Pat's sister Jan made a comment about it. I was there for the kids and no other reason.

After the first of the year, a discussion occurred in the master bedroom between Pat and me. She made reference to the death of Joseph Fielding Smith of the Mormon Presidency and the fact the Harold B. Lee was elevated to president the previous July. "That proves you are wrong in all of those dreams and visions you have had," she remarked.

"Not necessarily so," was my response. I felt the same spirit coming on me which I had experienced before. I said that if I were correct, Harold B. Lee would not live to see the end of that year (1973). "Oh please put that down on paper," she animated grabbing a pen and paper from the desk. I brushed it aside saying she was free to write down that Doug said such on that day. She didn't bother to. Again, my statement would later enlarge my dilemma.

Our conflicts and problems had no end. In March 1973, I received a telephone call at the office from Pat. I had a deposition to take in Vancouver and had gone down the street for lunch. Pat complained that there wasn't any food in the house for her to fix lunch and wanted me to come home. I explained my situation and told her she had a car and a checkbook. Then she screamed, "You get home or else!" Remembering the event of last fall, I agreed to go up to the house before driving down to Vancouver. As I drove in the driveway I saw Pat standing on the front porch with our son's 22 rifle pointed at me.

What she had in mind I didn't really know. She had demanded I come home and was now shouting at the top of her lungs for me to get out of there! Quickly I thought about the possibility of Jim having not shot off all the shells of his last purchase so there could be one in the chamber. I said to her, "There aren't any bullets in that gun." She said, "Try me!" I then told her to prove it;

point the gun at the ground and pull the trigger. She did just that. Hearing the "click" I took the rifle away from her.

Immediately, she rushed into the front hallway grabbing a wire coat hanger from the guest closet. Quickly she flattened in the sides so that she had a hook with which to inflict wounds on my face. I wrestled that away from her then she turned her fingernails sideways and slashed my face causing several open wounds and bleeding. After pushing her away, I went to the bathroom and applied alum and toilet tissue to stop the bleeding. Then I left and drove to the courthouse in Vancouver where I conducted a good deposition of a man attempting to gain custody of his 7-year-old daughter from my client. By that, time I had removed the tissue paper and having taken a bottle of make-up was able to conceal the wounds on my face.

The sister in the church for whom I was handling a divorce had called me earlier in the day about her divorce and concerns that her husband could never become a bishop in the Mormon Church if she went through with the divorce. I asked her why she would consider a marriage for time and all eternity if she couldn't stand it in this life. She grasped my point and told me to finalize the divorce.

On the way home, I decided it was time to take some of my own medicine. Thereafter, I drafted dissolution pleadings. I suggested an attorney for Pat. After negotiations, she would have custody of the minor children but Jim 16; Kevin 13 would live with me. Jennifer, then 8, would live with her. The two older girls were or would shortly be emancipated and in college. On July 5, 1973 the stressful 20 year marriage was over. Well, almost. There would be more stress for a while.

Chapter Seventeen

A New Relationship

During the mandatory waiting period for a divorce to run, I had met a woman in the course of my legal work on a child custody case; in fact the same case that I had to take a deposition the day Pat had sliced my face with her finger nails.

Darlene Ashbaugh was Director of nursing for a geriatrics nursing home in Vancouver, Washington. She was a friend of my client and a potential character witness in the custody dispute. I had interviewed her at work and was very impressed with her kindness and Christian wit and charm. Darlene had been married shortly after graduating from Deaconess Hospital in Spokane Washington. She had been divorced for about twelve years and had two daughters from her marriage.

We dated several times before my divorce was final. The gossip grapevine among the nursing profession had informed Pat of the connection. Before Pat completed the divorce by going to court in Stevenson, Washington, she had asked me about Darlene and was I going to marry her. At the time, I was feeling very good about Darlene and she had the same feeling for me, but I did not intend to marry again at least not right away.

Pat had been awarded the house in Portland and I kept the one in Woodland that had the entire hill sliding problems. Pat had legal custody of our two sons, solely for face saving purposes. It was agreed of course that the boys would live with me. Pat, however, made trips to my house, in my absence, bringing the boys baked goods and showering them with kindness in an attempt to lure them to live with her in Portland.

Within days of the divorce, our oldest son was feeling quite ill, perhaps under the influence of some debilitating substance. I undertook what in Mormonism is called "administering". That is, a blessing of healing given to the ill one to restore them to health and to remove any evil that they may be subject to. This is done

by use of consecrated olive oil and the laying on of hands in a two-part ritual. Usually it is done by two priesthood Holders (Elders). The timing was critical so I undertook it myself.

Within two days of that, I received a letter from Pat's attorney castigating me for pretending to "cast out the devil" from our son. Threats of going to court to enforce Pat's right to physical custody if I did not cease to practice witchcraft, etc. were made.

Pat kept calling the boys. They wanted me to stop her from doing so. She began to call Darlene and spend time in lengthy one-sided conversations about what kind of an evil person I was. One time I arrived at Darlene's to hear a little of such bad mouthing. I recall Darlene asking Pat why, if I was such a bad person, she wanted me back.

With Pat's pressure on both the boys and Darlene, I believed the sooner I married again, the better Pat would be cut off from that kind of harassment. After discussion with Darlene, we married later in the month of July.

The boys and I moved into Darlene's house. Ultimately I deeded the Woodland property back to the original owner as I gave up trying to rehabilitate it. Within a day or so of the new marriage, Pat appeared at the front door of Darlene's house. She insisted on talking to the boys. I told Kevin to talk to her. He did so, refusing her request to move to her home.

Thereupon she began to tear pictures and other items off the living room walls, tossing them to the floor. I picked her up and put her out the front door. Our daughter Cindy and her boyfriend had followed Pat over in an attempt to dissuade her from that insanity. They took control of her from that point and got her back to her home in Portland. Pat kept interfering with the boys for a year or so but lessened her assaults on Darlene and me.

Within a month I acquired a new house under construction and finished it off. Darlene and I, along with her two daughters and my two sons moved into it in time for school the fall of 1973. Later, my older son Jim would move out to live with his mother where he felt he had more freedom. He was sixteen. I had been pretty strict on him about his friends. Our younger son Kevin went to live with her also for a short while but returned to me where he stayed until he reached majority. He remembers Darlene as a caring mother.

In moving from the Woodland area, I had closed the law office there and rented an office in Vancouver where I offered space to Darrell Lee, a friend and former deputy prosecuting attorney from Kelso. Darrell was running for election as prosecuting attorney in Clark County against the "other attorney." Eventually Darrell would open a law office there and we would bring in two additional attorneys to share space.

After going through several legal secretaries in Woodland, I finally ended up with a bright young freckle faced girl, Sandy Rothschild, a year older than my daughter Teri. Sandy would relocate to Vancouver from the Kelso area to continue working for me and my associates. Sandy proved to be an excellent and loyal legal secretary.

Shortly before Christmas, 1973, I received a Christmas card from my missionary companion, Grant Hardy, with whom I had the serious discussion in September two years previous. He wanted to know how I now felt about Harold B. Lee. Lee had been installed as President of the Mormon Church in July of 1972 and the same person about whom Pat had made the comment earlier in 1973. I didn't reply until the day after Christmas.

I picked up the handset of my Dictaphone and dictated a letter to Grant in which I stated my belief that Lee was not a prophet of God. About 15 minutes to five, Sandy appeared at my desk with the letter to Grant. I was quite surprised and asked her how she got to it so fast. She mentioned that she had scanned ahead and listened to it. Knowing the subject matter was important to me, she decided to type it. I read it and signed it. She put it in the mail that evening. The date was December 26, 1973.

I had an appointment with a Mormon couple the following morning two days after Christmas. Following some small talk, he said, "Wasn't that a terrible thing that happened to Harold B. Lee last night". I hadn't heard and asked him what happened. Ecstatic he could give me some important news, he replied, "He died!"

I suddenly remembered my prophetic statement to Pat in the master bedroom earlier that year! I had said, "If I am correct he won't live to see the end of this year." David O. McKay died when I was deep in prayer about the issue of Black priesthood. Joseph Fielding Smith died on July 3, 1972 just short of the 30 months I had told my daughters Teri and Cyndi he would not live to if I were correct in my spiritual dilemma. Now this! Oh what do I do now? The couple in my office relating this information to me later told others that I was visibly shaken by the news. They had no idea of why.

I sent a Mail gram to Church authorities asking them to not install a new president without talking to me first. I wanted no responsibility for any more deaths! They of course ignored me, but I went through literal hell anyway!

A week or so later, Darrell came into my office with a confirmation letter from Western Union on the Mail gram I had sent. The confirmation had been sent to him based upon our telephone listing. He told me he respected my right to practice my religion but in no way did he want to become involved.

I told him he wouldn't. That was simply an error on the part of Western Union since his name was alphabetically first on our telephone listing. Suddenly, in my head the spirit of prophecy intervened. "You will be and you will make some money from it". I uttered. Later this prophetic statement would prove true.

At my insistence, Wally Teuscher made an effort to have a member of the Council of the Twelve confer with me at the next Stake conference in February 1974. The visitor was to be Howard Hunter. I painted an oil panting of Multnomah Falls located up the Columbia River Gorge from Portland. I had a brass plate engraved "Living Waters" which I attached to the frame.

116

At the appointed hour I placed the painting in the hallway outside the room in which the meeting was to take place. I waited in the chapel making a little one fingered music on the organ. In time, I was summoned to the meeting.

After introduction to Hunter, I asked them to wait as I went out to the hall and brought in the painting. Reaching down into the shipping crate to get it, I observed a look of fright on the face of Hunter and Wally as if maybe I was going to pull out a machine gun! The look of fright was replaced by a look of delight as I presented the painting to Hunter as a gift complete with shipping case.

We began a discussion. Hunter said, "What is this thing you are doing?" He had reference to an effort I had been making to find out what God had been intending me to do. I had created, at least on paper, an entity called the, Shiloh Society, with which I hoped to enlist the support of celebrities for a world peace movement. I explained that to him and he told me to stop doing that and to support the church in "Building up the Kingdom".

In Mormon doctrine, the word or title, "Apostle" means a "personal witness for Christ". Doctrine states that no one can be an apostle unless one has literally seen Christ. I asked Hunter if he had ever seen Christ. His face flushed red and he thrust his face away from me toward the wall exclaiming, "If I ever had, I would never tell a soul."

A small sized man, an undertaker in Las Vegas who was the Regional Representative of the Twelve, had accompanied Hunter to the Stake conference. He was in the room at the time. He was more or less jumping up and down shouting at me, "Brother Wallace, do you know who you are talking to?" I responded, "Yes an **impostor**"!

Hunter went on to say, "Brother Wallace, if you persist in this you will be destroyed!" Destroyed? Grant Hardy had said. "They will burn you!"

Some time later, after relating the experience to Darlene, she would have cause to say, "You allowed them to intimidate you."

Beginning in the winter of 1974, I made it a policy to spend at least one Sunday a month visiting my father in Salem, Oregon. He and mother lived immediately south of the Salem Stake Center building. He had become a confidant to many members of the church who would stop by and chat. He kept up on the latest and most current gossip.

On one of those visits, at the supper table, he asked what were those pieces of jewelry being given out to the Home Teachers. My first response was, "Oh no they aren't starting that are they?" Then I added, "They are not being given to everyone are they?" He replied in the negative. I then told him what I knew about it.

On May 3, 1974, Darlene gave birth to a son whom we named Darren Alan. My initials of course were DAW. Darlene's were DAW and now our son would be DAW.

In August of 1974, we rented a motor home in which we took dad and mother Wallace along with Darlene's daughter Sherry and my son Kevin and of course Darren just three months old, on a trip in Oregon. We first stopped at Oakridge where dad had built a home on a steep hillside back in the late 30's. Then on to Diamond Lake where we spent the night. The next morning it was off to Crater Lake. Dad and mother had lived in Oregon for 36 years but never made a visit to those popular tourist sites.

The elevation at Crater Lake was too much for dad's breathing and heart so we moved on to the Oregon Caves. I stayed in the motor home with him and baby Darren while everyone else including mother, then 76, went on the two-hour tour of the caves.

Several years before, while staying at my sister Jean's home during the summer 1970 I had first told dad about the spiritual things I had experienced. Over the succeeding years, he would query me about those experiences. Again, in the motor home he wanted know more. He looked me in the eyes and asked the question, "Did those things really happen to you?" "Yes Dad, they did", was my reply. He then said he believed me, as I had never lied to him. I told him there was one time when I did but only that one time. He admonished me to follow the directions given me in those experiences.

118

To those members of my family who have criticized my later actions in regard to the church, I would remind them such actions were the result of approval of grand-dad Wallace albeit neither he, nor I knew at the time what those actions would be.

Each October mother and my sister Muriel would travel to Utah to do genealogical research in the church offices. This would happen during October semi-annual conference of the church. In the fall of 1974, I asked mother if she would stop by the old Lincoln Grade school to see if it was still there. I had been having a haunting of the mind about it because of the event that happened in 1937. She said she would do that for me.

Upon her return, she informed me that a new school had been built, so she didn't go by the old school. The next year she would go by the old school grounds and report to me what she saw.

In the fall of 1974, I began to phase out the practice of law. I had taken on two modular home distributorship's and was concentrating on that more than the practice. I would eventually sell my books and furniture to associates who shared the office. I felt a need to get out of the practice because of a feeling of an impending assault on church doctrines and practices. I knew I would be vulnerable had I remained active in law. By the summer of 1975, I was pretty well involved in construction only.

As it turned out later, a great deal of effort would be made by agents of the church to get me back into practice. I will detail that effort later.

Chapter Eighteen

The Passing of the Patriarch

The frustration of my spiritual dilemma continued even after Dad had given me his blessing to proceed as I would be directed. The problem was that there was not any current direction. Feeling alone, I decided to make another approach to the new President of the church, Spencer W. Kimball.

In May 1975, I flew to Salt Lake City and checked into a hotel. I called the office of Kimball and was connected to D. Arthur Haycock, the personal secretary to Kimball. Identifying myself, I asked if I could set up an appointment to speak to someone who had the ear of President Kimball.

"Oh, Brother Wallace, yes, you paint oil paintings do you not?" I knew then that my interview with Howard Hunter of the Twelve a year earlier had been discussed. I answered in the affirmative. He then said he thought that Brother Hunter had resolved my questions at that interview. I told him that had not occurred. He then said he would be happy to meet me at 9:am. the next morning.

At the appointed hour I was present in the front lobby of the old church headquarters building in which I had worked some twenty four years earlier. Haycock was notified of my presence and after shaking hands he led me toward the rear right of the building to his office, just next to the office of the church president.

He invited me to sit at his desk. Before I was allowed to speak, he put his hand up for me to be quiet as he dialed a 4 digit inside number. As he was doing so, I noticed a glitter coming from a pin on the lapel of his suit. I looked closely and recognized it as the BEE lapel pin I had heard of several years earlier. I knew I was being recorded somewhere within the church building complex. His words were, "Yes, it is all set you can proceed now."

After he hung up and indicated I could talk, I said, "Wow, that's an unusual piece of jewelry you are wearing." He replied, "Yes it is nice isn't it?" I asked him where he got it and he responded, "From the Church in recognition of my many years of service." That was the stock answer I had been told would be given to anyone who would inquire about it.

We talked about my dilemma. I did not tell him everything by any means. Oddly, we were interrupted twice. Once by a telephone call from a Stake or Mission President of the church in Brazil*. The other was the unannounced appearance of Spencer W. Kimball!

The telephone call was a discussion of the denial of priesthood to a black man. The question asked of Haycock appeared to be; "to what degree away from a black progenitor must a male be to be able to be ordained to the priesthood"?

Haycock's answer was severe. That <u>any,</u> "black blood" in the ancestry of the candidate would disqualify him for ordination. I said nothing. Later during our conversation, Haycock looked behind me and said, "President, this is Brother Wallace." I stood up turning and there by the door was President Kimball. He was a short man somewhat stocky with a husky voice; I believe the result of throat cancer. * *Prior edition contained error of Hawaii.*

We both stepped forward and shook hands. He looked up at me and was visibly shaking at the introduction. He indicated to Haycock that he had to leave the meeting he was in to gather some papers on his desk that was needed.

After our introduction, he went into his office. The door was wide open and I could see into it. Kimball never approached his desk but turned where he appeared to stand behind the wall. Haycock and I continued our conversation. About five minutes later, Kimball appeared again going out the same door he had come in. But he had no papers in his hand.

I admit that during the conversation with Haycock my eyes welled up with tears. Years of pent up emotion had burst over the wall of restriction. I may have appeared to be a weeping fool!

Haycock then directed me to go upstairs to the office of LeGrand Richards. Richards, you will recall had been my Boss when I worked for the church 24 years earlier. He also officiated at my temple wedding with Pat twenty-two years earlier. Richards, you will also recall, was the General Authority with whom I had exchanged correspondence in 1972 during the time of the death of President Joseph Fielding Smith. He was also to tell me that he thought the other "Brethren" would have believed him simple had he brought up the issue of my personal dilemma at that time.

Consternation showed on the face of Richard's secretary. She led me into Richard's office. There seated behind a desk was a shaking, trembling old man. "Why are you doing these things," he asked. "Why don't you stop it and help build up the kingdom?" I assured him that I was no threat to anyone. I asked him a few questions and he began to calm down.

Richards had written a book about Jews and Mormonism. He was regarded as an expert on the issue of the conversion of Jews to Mormonism. He offered me a piece of information that, Kimball upon becoming the President and Prophet of the church, had asked him to outline what he, Kimball, was supposed to be doing about the church and Israel! The thought crossed my mind; "The Prophet is asking a mortal, not God for these answers?"

I took leave of Richards and returned to my hotel. That afternoon, I flew back to Portland. I had not resolved anything about my dilemma. However, the trip gave me a little insight. I saw the first use of the BEE spy system against me. I learned that my name had been discussed at the highest levels of the church. I witnessed fear on the face of both Kimball and Richards at our initial meeting.

The following Sunday, I visited dad in Salem. He was very anxious to tell me that since my visit to Kimball, he had been approached by priesthood authorities to accept a BEE lapel pin. He told them he wasn't a Home Teacher and he didn't want it.

They told him it was being offered to him because he had put in so many years of service to the church.

"Of course you wouldn't want to wear it all the time! Perhaps just when your son Douglas visits you. You could proudly display it then," They said.

Dad refused it. I expressed disappointment, but was glad he did, as it could have been more of a problem than we could have handled at the time. I will later detail more use of it against me and my finally, learning its technology in 1979.

A week or two later, I again visited Dad. It seemed each time I would barely get in the house before he would have a question for me. This time he asked, "The spy system. What part of the earth does it cover?" I responded, "North and South America. Potentially the whole earth." Again, "What problems did they have in installing the system?" I responded again by the spirit, "A blank area where they could not send out a signal. But they fixed it." "Where," he asked. My mind scanned the Pacific Northwest. "Here, from the bottom of the Willamette Valley to Mt. St Helens in Washington: from the Coast Range to the Cascades," was my reply.

"How", he asked. "By installing a booster tower," I again responded. "Where," he asked. "In the Oregon City- Redlands area," I said. With that he slapped his hand on his knee and said, **"I'll be damned!"** His grapevine at the church next door had informed him of the problem the church had encountered when testing the system after its initial installation. Everything I said was not from knowledge gleaned from any source except the spirit at the moment he had asked. This made Dad even more convinced I should do as the spirit directed me. Later In 1978, the existence of the presence of microwave transmissions in the Willamette Valley became local headlines.

Less than three months later, Dad was taken ill with heart failure. We moved him from Physicians and Surgeons Hospital in Portland to the Hill Haven Nursing Home in Vancouver,

Washington, where Darlene was administrator. He was slowly dying. His lungs were filling with liquid. On the 17th day of August 1975, an alert of no pulse or blood pressure was given. I was at his side. He asked me, "What is happening." I told him everything was okay and held his hand as he slipped into unconsciousness. We moved him back to the hospital in Portland where he quietly passed over to the other side.

A month later, I went through the grieving process. This began a period of six weeks of depression for me. Now that dad was gone, I felt the pressure on me to perform what ever tasks my spiritual dilemma would guide me. Dad had given me his blessings before he died. Not to proceed now would have made me feel dishonest to him. Since he was somewhat of a racist, what I would be called upon to do would not have pleased him were he alive. David O. McKay and Alec Wallace had passed on. The two men in my life that would have caused me to hesitate were no longer impeding my response to the Spirit. The issue of Black priesthood would soon loom large on the World's television screens. However, at this time I did not know such would be the case

Chapter Nineteen

A Night of Direction

Some would say, **"Ah ha, It is of the Devil, just look at the time it came,"** October 31, 1975, Halloween. Being still in a depression over the death of my father, and the stalemate of my spiritual dilemma, I went from the bedroom I shared with Darlene to the living room to spend the balance of the night. I meditated all those things that had been bothering me.

Around midnight or shortly thereafter, thoughts began popping into my mind in a pattern I was familiar with. It was time to cease asking church leaders for help and direction. It was time to seek direction from God! In most positive terms, I was to challenge the leaders to respond. They would have a time certain, a time definite in which they sit down with me and discuss all items of concern or I would be free from subordination and proceed as I was personally directed by God. In the likely event that they did not respond, I would give them notice of insubordination. I did not know what would happen. I did not know anything beyond an assurance I would be directed each step, as it became necessary.

My heart was lifted! I was now running on the see-thru tires of faith! I thanked God, for I now had a plan of procedure. It did not come from me, but came from on high. I spent the rest of the night on the couch returning to the bedroom at daybreak. I related this uplifting information to Darlene. She was so happy to see me in high spirits again!

This day was Saturday; Darlene was a consultant for a woman by the name of Betty Moretti. Betty owned a licensed group facility in Vancouver. Washington. She also had a nursing home in Lebanon, Oregon which she had purchased in a state of decay and decline. It appeared that Betty was re-furbishing that facility. She had asked Darlene to paint an oil painting to hang on her office wall.

Darlene had a meeting with Betty that day. She brought her landscape painting to me to see if I could make the creek water come alive. I was able to do that for her and she was off to her meeting where she would present the oil to Betty.

I spent the day composing a letter to the President of the Mormon Church. I used a style of revelation. A, "Thus saith the Lord," style for indeed that was the manner in which I had received it. The direction was from Him not me. I was only a messenger.

In that letter, I placed Spencer Wooley Kimball on notice that he had until January 1, 1976 to confer with me. If he failed to do so then I would be free to proceed as the Lord directed. I had no idea at this time what the procedure would be after January 1st.

I must remind the reader that at this stage of my life experiences, I had no reason to doubt the authenticity of the beginnings of the church. I believed it was divinely brought forth through the instrumentality of Joseph Smith, Jr. Therefore, the bias of my own mind put words into the mouth of God. At this time, and shortly afterward, I used the term, "My servant, Joseph Smith." Later, when my eyes were open to the true history of the church, it would have been impossible for me to have written such a thing! This points out flaws, which exist within scriptures written by man. They attempted to relate spiritual experiences which they may have had but could perceive only as the bias of their mind allowed!

Later that same day, I noticed Darlene drive the van into the circular driveway in front of the house. She was followed by another car, upon entering the vestibule; Darlene introduced me to Betty Moretti, and was off to the bedroom. Betty was a rather short woman in her early sixties. As we shook hands, she trembled. I asked her if she were cold, to which she replied in a positive voice, " Oh no!" Later, she would remind me of that experience and explain why she had trembled. It was because she had "seen" that moment before. In the next few months, I would have dealings with Betty that were to say the least a little disconcerting.

Shortly before the event of November 1st, I had another con-conversation with mother about the Ogden grade school. She had been to church conference again in October and visited the former site of the school. "It is torn down, just rock ruble where the school used to be," she said. "Is the play ground still there," I asked. She replied, "Yes, the chain link fence but the asphalt is cracked with weeds coming through it," she added.

I was elated because that is where the experience on my eighth birthday occurred. I also told mother about a recent dream in which I had gone up a street by the new Ogden Temple to an old abandoned irrigation canal and pointed back to the temple telling God it was okay to destroy it! "Why would you do that?" She asked. I could not answer.

During the month of November 1975, I wrote a letter to D. Arthur Haycock, the male secretary to President Kimball. I made several suggestions about improving church posture. I found that later, some of those suggestions had been implemented. I sent a colored photograph of a painting I had made of a 1968 dream. This picture was of an arched structure located over the Dome of the Rock* in Jerusalem. Haycock responded that the church was studying it. No further contact was made with church Authorities until January 1976. *[In January 2000, I placed a website on the internet with that painting as a home page under title of worldpeaceministry.org.]

The first of the year came and passed without any response from Salt Lake. I then composed a letter to President Kimball in which I informed him that his failure to respond to me by January 1st freed me from being under control of church leaders and that I was free to proceed with my agenda as God would direct. What that agenda was I had no clue. However, that letter triggered a definite knee jerk reaction from Salt Lake City that found its way into my living room in Vancouver, Washington.

Chapter Twenty

Busy Bees

It was the first Sunday in January 1976. A very bold knock came at the front Door. I went to the door and opened it. There stood my assigned Home Teachers, Roy King and his son-in-law. This was unusual because Roy hardly ever did his home teaching. At least that had been my experience in the two plus years living in that residence. I welcomed them into the house.

As I closed the door behind them, my eyes were drawn to the very large golden BEE lapel pins each of them wore. These pieces of jewelry were vulgarly large. Like the size of a political button, you might see on the lapel of a person in support of some candidate for public office.

Instantly, I knew what they were and quickly surmised the purpose of the unexpected visit. I said,"Wow those are interesting pieces of jewelry! Where did you get them?" The response of course was stock. "We received them from the church in recognition of our many years of service to the church."

I invited them to sit down. Normally, a spiritual message would be given followed by requests of how they could be of service to the family or me. *Not this time!*

"Brother Wallace, You have been writing letters to Salt Lake City in which you threaten to take measures into your own hands," Roy stated. Then he asked, "Who are the people that support you and what is it you intend to do?"

The loudness of this inquisition was sufficient to cause Darlene to come out of the kitchen with a look of terror on her face as she stood in the archway to the living room. She looked at me, then Roy, and his son-in-law. I gave her a wave off signal to let her know I had the situation under control.

"Yes, Brother Roy, I have written letters to Salt Lake. In fact, a number of letters over the past 4 years. Wally Teuscher and Orson Arnold (The new Stake President) are well aware of it. If you need to know, go ask them what it is all about, "I immediately replied.

I added that it was a personal matter between the church president and me. I would not discuss it with him. As to identifying my supporters, I told him I didn't have any. I also said I had no idea what I would be doing if in fact anything. I would just leave it up to the Lord.

Seeing they weren't getting anywhere with me, they bid goodbye without any kind of a spiritual or uplifting message. They were on an intelligence mission and failed: so out the door they went!

Darlene and I discussed the nature of the interrogation that had typical Mormon priesthood arrogance. I guess I didn't understand the persistence the church would apply in their endeavor to discover what I would be doing in the future. It is amusing to reflect on the situation. They had all the opportunity in the world for two full months to sit down and openly discuss matters with me. They refused to do that and now they were using Home Teachers, of all persons, to find out what they could have perhaps known earlier.

Darlene and I had produced a number of oil paintings which we were to soon show in the lobby of an area hospital. The next morning, I was doing a little preparatory touch up on one of the paintings when the telephone rang. The caller was Pat. She wanted to know if I was busy. I told her what I was doing but I could talk with the telephone propped on my shoulder.

"No, I don't mean that. I want you to come over so that we can talk about some problems, I am having with the kids." she said.

At this time, Jennifer age 10, and Jimmy age 18 were living with her. I could not imagine what kind of problems she was having that could not be discussed on the telephone.

After some discussion about being able to get away at that time, I agreed to come over for a few minutes, I called Darlene and told her what was up, that I was going over to Pat's but would be back in time to have lunch with her.

"Coming" or **"Going over"**, meant a least a 35 minute drive from Vancouver, Washington, over the Columbia River to Portland and then a drive to South East Bush Street where Pat lived.

Upon arriving I could see Pat standing in the dining area of the house. She saw me and beckoned me in. This was the same house we had lived in together for ten years before moving to Woodland. I walked to the back of the house. She moved away from me and began," Doug, who are these people that follow you and what is it you are planning on doing with the church?"

My response was that it was none of her business. We had divorced in part because she wouldn't allow me to be my own person and follow the dictates of my conscience. "Well, I know that, but I am still interested," She added.

As she talked, she moved toward the sliding glass door. The sunlight streaming through it caught a reflection on her white blouse. Looking closer, I saw it was the smallest of the BEE lapel pins! The same size that D. Arthur Haycock had worn in his

office almost a year earlier.

I said to her," Isn't that a nice piece of jewelry! That is only being given out to "Elders", (Mormon priesthood) how come you have one on this morning?" Her response was, "Perhaps this is a way of the church showing me I still have priesthood even though we are divorced!" I admonished her to get rid of it as all those who have been involved with it will one day regret it. She wanted to know how I knew that and I told her to look it up in the scriptures: something about arrows being shot directly to the beast.

At this point, I asked her how her love life was. This I could do because she had earlier confided in me with information about a member of the church whom she had been seeing. No sooner did I ask that question than she quickly left the room heading for her bedroom with a statement that there was something she had to do! I heard her talking. Spinning around I looked at the telephone on the kitchen wall. There was no way she had time to dial a telephone. I then knew she was using the BEE lapel pin as a microphone. Upon re-entering the dining room, her blouse was minus the pin. I commented on that to which she replied she didn't want to always wear it.

I again admonished her to get rid of it and took leave. Not one word about the children had been spoken although that was the ostensible reason I had spent over an hour driving! I had lunch with Darlene and related the adventure to her. Darlene had that look of being sadly concerned at such things.

About two weeks later, Jennifer came over to my house to spend the weekend. Taking Jeni home Sunday evening, I went into the house to see what Pat had done about the lapel pin. When I asked her if she still had the pin she threw her arms up in the air saying, "I gave it back. I told them I didn't want anything to do with it."

After leaving Pat's home, I went over to visit Earl Wiest. I gave him a Time-Life book which featured the history of the Dome of the Rock in Jerusalem. We had talked about that subject a lot in our days of fishing. I asked him where was his jewelry? Of course, I had reference to the BEE lapel pin. He looked at me and said," Doug, I told you I would never have anything to do with it!" In spite of their sophisticated technology, the knee jerk reaction from Salt Lake had failed to enlighten church security forces.

Chapter Twenty One

Black Priesthood from the Lord

For many years as an adult Gospel Doctrine teacher in the Mormon Church, I would often say, "Some day I am going to find myself a solid wall about fifty feet long and ten feet high." What I meant by that was I wanted to write scriptures on a wall and then link them together to form indisputable proof that the gospel was true and mankind had been given all that was necessary for him to re-member himself with God.

The Hill Haven Nursing Home in Vancouver, Washington where Darlene was Administrator had such a wall. I discovered it one day when I went to the basement area where the laundry was located along with the janitorial room.

Asking permission, I obtained white butcher paper which I hung on the wall two rows high so that I could take a felt pen and list scores of scriptures that were related to one another. Finally, there was proof positive aligning itself for me.

I would work on the project for a few minutes or longer each day as the spirit guided. I wondered what the laundry personnel might think of it but that didn't deter me. The product of that exercise is an unpublished work titled, "We Three, Satan 'n God 'n Me.

Sometime in February or early March, I became aware of a young black man about 22 years of age working as a janitor in the facility, I asked Darlene who that was. She told me his name was Larry Lester and she had interviewed him for a temporary job as a janitor. She said she hired him because he seemed to her to be an all-American boy.

Later, I would learn from Larry, that he was actually a machine operator for Jantzen Knitting Mills in Portland. He had been laid off for a short period while new machinery was installed in the mills. He told me that as he went past Hill Haven, something said to him go in there and ask for a job. Larry had learned in his youth to follow such promptings whenever they happened to him. He didn't need a job and had never been a janitor but accepted the challenge for what it was.

One morning in March 1976, Larry came to me as I worked on the wall. I had spoken very little to him before that time. He said he had been looking at my writings on the wall and they made a lot of sense to him. He wanted to know if he stayed after work in the mornings could he and I talk about it? It also seems that the Lord had led Larry to Portland from Southern California where he had attended a Christian Seminar. He said he had been told to go north where he could become a priest before God!

I agreed and he and I would discuss religion, including Mormonism several times a week. Early one morning I had a prompting of the spirit to ask Larry if he would allow me to Baptize and ordain him a priest. Before I could say anything to him, he told me he knew what I was going to ask. He said he knew that I wanted to ordain him a priest before God. How did he know that? He said the spirit told him that night.

As to Mormonism, Larry had no conviction; He followed the teachings of Christ wherever he found them. He believed the church of God was much bigger and greater than institutional religion. Larry was and is a great human being.

My own convictions of Mormonism were fading as I began to realize that the church was in so much error. I also saw error in many of the Christian churches. The attitudes of living called the Beatitudes as outlined by Christ on the Mount went far beyond doctrinal walls of organized religion and were applicable to anyone at any time.

Larry agreed to partake of the priesthood ordination. I scheduled the event for the second day of April 1976. I was led to engage a small public relations firm to arrange the details. They had it set up for the Travelodge Motor Inn on Broadway in N. E. Portland Oregon.

In the evening of April 1st, they notified the media and the local leaders of the Mormon Church what I would be doing. The Travelodge opened and heated its swimming pool for the occasion.

The sinister side of Mormonism began its appearance the next morning. Darlene had dated a much older medical doctor some years before she and I met. He had proposed marriage to her but she declined because of his age. She felt her life would be tied up taking care of him.

This doctor was a Mormon. No sooner had Darlene shown up for work than this man called attempting to persuade her to meet him at the Red Lion Motor Inn on Hayden Island for a day of hanky panky. She told him she was married but that didn't seem to stop him. Here was first proof of the existence of dossiers which the church assembles on persons they consider a threat in order to allow them to make a pre-emptive strike against those persons. This was a part of the BEE spying system. Darlene was not a Mormon, but since she was married to me, they learned all they could about her to use against me if they could.

Darlene of course declined but wanted to tell me about it as soon as I appeared at Hill Haven for a brief interview by a reporter from the Columbian Newspaper. At that interview I learned that Stake President, Orson Arnold, had attempted to dissuade the media from giving the planned event any coverage by a statement that I had, "prophesied" that the church president would die and he hadn't. I was asked about that and said yes; I did for the prior leaders who had died within the parameters I had given.

I had asked two friends of mine, aviator John Evans, and Marion Wright to be participants in the event. After, I ordained Larry; He would in turn baptize and ordain Marion a priest. Little attention was ever given to that by the media or the church. We arrived at the Travelodge some half-hour before the scheduled event.

The first two people to arrive were the Area Public Relations Officer for the church and a companion. The large golden BEE lapel pins they were wearing easily identified both of these men. They wore the pins during the press conference inside of the building but took them off outside where television crews and photographers were active.

The media showed up in unexpectedly large numbers. The three local newspapers were there together with Associated Press and other smaller weekly papers. All Portland television channels were present. I spoke at the microphone for about fifteen minutes outlining my displeasure with discrimination within the Mormon Church. I related it as a life long concern. I stated I was an ordained High Priest of the church and I was taking it upon myself to break this damnation.

After my address, we retired to the outside swimming pool area where the rituals were to be preformed. However, one of the Mormon agents came to me before we retired to the outside. He wanted to be able to use the microphone to tell another version of the event that day. I told him,"No," he could hold his own press conference later. Thereafter he and his partner went about attempting to dissuade the media from giving the event publicity.

What a mistake that was! The media grabbed on the event that day in a feeding frenzy! The element of controversy was all they needed to make the story fly!

As it turned out, there was not another newsworthy event that day in the world which would overshadow the ordination of a Black man in the Mormon Church. Oddly, neither the church nor the media grasped a reality that occurred. Larry Lester was not baptized in the Mormon Church nor was he ordained a "priest" in the church. Had they grasped that truth, history might have turned out differently. For the moment, the world was alive with the headlines, "Mormons Ordain First Black."

Doug Wallace ordains Larry Lester as Marion Wright waits to be baptized.

Validity of ceremony questioned

Mormons ordain first black

Headlines happened all over the world

April 2nd and 3rd, 1976

Baptismal Protest (PORTLAND) Marion L. Wright, left, is baptized by Larry Lester in the swimming pool of a Portland motel. Douglas Wallace, right, later ordained Lester as a member of the Aaronic Priesthood in the Latter-day Saints Church, an act forbidden by church authorities. (AP)

Mormon Law Challenged; Black Ordained as Priest

Marion Wright is baptized by Larry Lester

The media and the Mormon Church failed to

Consider the significance of this act

Chapter Twenty Two

Repression Broken!

Saturday April 3, 1976 was a day of telephone activity. I received responses of support from many parts of the country. The media continued to play up the event. One call I had was from a brother in the church who lived in The Tri-Cities area of Washington. He spoke of Ogden, also the town of his birth. He mentioned that the Mormon elite always regarded Ogden as a second rate community. In fact, he was very emotional in discussing it. He offered me support and thanks for having the boldness to do what he felt should have been done many years earlier.

The local church attempted to down play the event and to discredit me with statements like Wallace hadn't attended church much in recent months and he hadn't been paying his tithing. Such comments should of course never be made. However, as I was soon to learn, the church will always attempt to discredit a person before dealing directly with the merits of an issue.

On Sunday, April 4th, I received a telephone call from a television reporter from Salt Lake City, Lucky Severson. He was in Portland at the Travelodge and wanted to interview me saying he sensed something larger was present in the ordination. I met with him on the deck around the pool where the ordination of Larry had taken place two days earlier. I answered most of his questions but was evasive about my immediate plans. I did recognize him as a person I had seen in my dreams.

April 6th is the day the church was officially organized. Every year, annual conferences of the church are held close to that date or on the date if possible. The conference will generally occupy three days beginning on Friday and ending on Sunday, This year, the 6th was on Tuesday. The church would hold the closing sessions on Tuesday.

It was my plan to travel to Salt Lake City and to make an appearance at the conference. I intended to take the issue of black priesthood right to the podium of the Tabernacle.

In the weeks preceding this event I had a dream in which I saw myself, in the company of friends, attempting to make an approach to the podium in the tabernacle but being lifted up and carried backward away from the podium.

I also had a dream in which I would be allowed to address the conference at a time when the church would disavow further pursuit of the physical, "Kingdom of God on Earth" agenda with its leader as earth "King".

I did not know which of these dreams would be a reality this day, if either of them. All I could do was to look for signs that would allow me to know which one.

I met with Lucky Severson again early on Monday at the Travelodge. This time in the company of both John and Marion. Since I had seen in a dream a successful encounter on Temple Square, I also had a precognition of Lucky being present at the North gate of the square in the context of that successful mission. It became imperative for me to ask him a question in connection with that successful event for he would be the one who would take control of television cameras by switching from church owned KSL television to his station to broadcast to the world, the events taking place in the Tabernacle

So, in the presence of both John and Marion, I posed a question to him. Would he be prepared to do just that tomorrow in Salt Lake City? He left us for a time to confer with his boss and came back with a negative answer. This should have alerted me to the fact that the trip tomorrow would prove to be the negative one, but undaunted I proceeded. Lucky later became a national TV personality and was stationed in Japan for a time. If what I have seen of the future is correct, he will yet play a role in educating the world to the evil nature of Mormonism.

My Friends, John Evans, Marion Wright and his wife Sharon, along with Darlene accompanied me in our van to Salt Lake City on Monday April 5th. We drove from Portland arriving In Ogden at 2:00 am.

On the way, I had the feeling that a death had occurred. My first thought was it was Kimball. That was not confirmed by the spirit. I said, "No not Kimball, but someone has died." Later we turned on the car radio to learn that Howard Hughes had died and his body was flown to Houston TX. In the not too distant future that would prove an interesting event, as I became drawn into the circumstance surrounding the Mormon connection with Hughes!

Our intention was to check into a large motel room and to get some sleep so that we could be up and on the road to Salt Lake City in time for the 10:00 am. session of conference.

As we drove down Washington Blvd. in Ogden, we passed the Temple. The lights were shining upon it and indeed, it looked beautiful. We obtained a large room in the Holiday Inn where we all slept in our clothes. All except me. As I lay there trying to sleep, I found myself arguing with God about the Temple. It was so beautiful; I argued why does it have to be destroyed?

Suddenly from a far, I had a vision of myself bowing to a white stone! "Satan...you b--------d, get away from me," I exclaimed. Immediately I knew I had to make that trip up the hill which I had seen in the dream I told mother about the previous October.

I told Darlene and my friends I had to go out on a short journey. I drove the van north on Washington Blvd. to the intersection at the south corner of the temple block, from there I turned east. There was a misty rain with overcast skies.

Just I had seen in the dream, the street ended at a hillside, but I could see a muddy trail ahead of me, which veered to the left. I followed that trail and it took me alongside an empty irrigation canal as I had seen in that same dream.

I got out of the van and stood by the side of it. Down below me was a child waiting for a school bus. He had a lunch pail and was looking up at me. In my dream, I had also looked up at myself from the same vantage point that the child was standing. I had seen myself the same as if through that child's eyes. I looked to the West. There, in a small break of the clouds, the sun poured through lighting up the golden Angel Moroni atop the tower of the temple,

I bowed my head and engaged in prayer to God. "I know not why, but destroy that building if you will," I said. At that moment, a view of the old Lincoln Grade School flashed into my mind and I knew this was the moment to visit the abandoned school grounds.

I managed to find my way onto 7th Street past the house where my young friends had set upon me some 38 years earlier. I drove past our childhood home at 657. Then down to the corner where the old 8th Ward building stood. I turned right and headed up the street towards the former school grounds.

As I approached it on my left, I saw there was just ruble where the building footprint had been as mother had said. The playground was infested with weeds in the cracks of the asphalt. The chain link fence was still there.

A very light rain was settling on the van's windshield. The wipers were slowly swishing back and forth. I bowed my head to meditate. Suddenly in my mind appeared white carved buildings on a black background! "Oh my God," I exclaimed, "That is when it happened"

On page 17 of this book, I chronicled a series of events that led me to the moment I was now freeing from repression of the event that had occurred on May 8, 1937. You will recall I had sworn at the Eighth Ward church building," God, I know you are in there...How come..?" After that, I had ridden my cycle down the street and into the school grounds. Just as I got past the school building, a flash of light to my left caused me to dump the machine and my presence of mind appeared back at the volleyball net. Behind the net, I saw a small personage suspended in the air that I called out to, "Michael"! I knew him! He was my friend, my confidant. I was overjoyed! I attempted to speak to him but his finger went to his mouth. Shush, was the message, and I listened as best an 8 year old could understand.

"I heard your prayer" were words that came to me; *"I Am not a God of stone, steel, brick, mortar, or glass! I dwell not in structures made by the hand of man! I dwell only in the hearts of those who know and love me!"*

The voice went on, *"Through the centuries, men have created beautiful structures to lure the masses into a belief that I dwell in them. Because they have built these works of art, they encourage people to look to them, the builders for permission to find me in those structures, but I cannot be found therein. Those who would place themselves as special agents between my people and me deceive their followers."*

"In this valley are men who have falsely set themselves up as my priesthood. They claim special favors with me and cloak themselves in the trappings of religion. In doing this, they deceive many. They build structures they call temples and encourage a belief among their followers that I dwell in them. In this way, these men obtain blind obedience of their followers. In my own time I will destroy all of these!"

At this moment, a panorama of white buildings in the design of Mormon temples on a black velvet-like background; was passed before my mind's eye. These buildings were like carvings of white Ivory soap. <u>This associated scene would overcome repression 39 years later!</u>

The voice went on,*" My people in this valley are special to me. They have beseeched their leaders for a temple to be built here. I have not allowed that. In time, as they become more worldly, their leaders will yet build such a building for them. Those*

142

leaders tell their followers that the highest leader among them is to be crowned earth king to rule the world for a thousand years for me. It is an evil I will not allow to happen.

You are among those who have been called to prevent that catastrophe upon the earth. You will not need to research this for I have called many others to that task. You will use that information to lead my people out of the bondage of these men."

"When will this happen," I asked. *"You need not concern yourself for it will come about naturally as you are guided by the spirit,"* came a reply that added, *"When the people have a temple in Ogden, that will be the time when you will commence your work."* My mind was alive with inquisitiveness. "But how old will I be," I asked. *"You will be in your late forties,"* was the answer.

This event then closed and I heard a girl calling me by name, "Doug, Doug, are you alright?" I heard her but I could not see her. She led me home by the hand as I guided my cycle along. For years, I thought this was Janine Cardingly, a girl whom I had a crush on who lived just down the street from me. Janine had been in a fire and had horrible burn scars on her back.

Years later, in fact on New Year's eve, just three months earlier before this recall, My sister Jean and I were reminiscing our childhood in Ogden when she piped up, "Hey Doug remember that time when those boys beat you up and you went down to the grade school and I found you there?

"Was that you," I had asked! It was a shock to learn after 38 years that Jean was the one who led me home.

Had I not been blind at the time, I would have known it was she. However this day was now April 6th, 1976 and I had an urgent mission to perform.

After this recall, I felt very humble for all of the things that had occurred to me in my life. I now understood why the various spiritual events had happened. They were a training for me for a mission yet to be fulfilled.

As I drove south on Washington Blvd, I passed the Ogden temple again. It took some courage but I raised my hand pointing at it and again repeated my words to God "Destroy it as you will." Temples no longer would have value in my life.

There now was a sense of direction and purpose. It was not just the issue of black equality in the eyes of God; there was an evil in Mormon Church leaders seeking political control of the earth. I now knew I must resist that agenda which I had in fact supported for many years. This began for me an experience with the sinister side of Mormonism.

Chapter Twenty Three

The Lord's Work Rejected

Returning to the motel, our group prepared for the trip to Salt Lake City and the annual conference of the church. I had prepared a manuscript which I thought was important to have with me. That manuscript briefly outlined my spiritual experiences as I have related to this point in this book. I needed to have a black thin loose-leaf binder for it which I had not been able to buy before leaving Portland.

Darlene volunteered for the mission of getting one. I was amazed at how fast she returned with it. She has her own story to tell of miracles about how she was led to find it. That in itself is very unusual for a binder that thin is a rarity.

Darlene attempted to find out what would happen at the tabernacle. I told her only about the successful scene. I told her about going through the north gate of temple square to be met by many supporters, who would say, "Make way for the Lord!" "Careful", she responded, thinking maybe all this was getting to my head. I told her I wouldn't be saying it, the supporters would and they had reference to my being on a mission for the Lord, not me personally. She then understood.

In the back of my mind, the weather was not compatible with the successful venture into temple square for it was overcast with rain threatening as we stopped at the north gate of temple square. I made the comment that this did not look right for it was a bleak deserted scene, yet there were things that beckoned me to proceed.

Since we were double parked, I asked Darlene to drive the van east about three blocks on North Temple to a parking lot and then return to the square. I felt she would be safer and would not witness any harsh or unpleasant things that might happen.

I asked Sharon to go into the tabernacle and ascend the north side balcony, seating herself as close toward the front of the building as possible. I knew John, Marion and I would enter from the south side of the tabernacle at approximately an alignment with the podium.

For this occasion, I had purchased a white Panama suit which I wore, together with a white tie, belt and shoes. John and Marion each wore white sweaters, white shirt and shoes. To those who ask why, I can only answer, as did Abraham when he offered Isaac up for sacrifice, "I know not why except that the Lord God has commanded it," was his response. In my case this day I had seen us wearing white and accepted that as God's direction.

Since it was a dark overcast day, some man on Temple Square who saw us, shouted out a comment about our white clothing being out of place. However, when we were inside, there was no mistake about seeing us. Oddly just a few hundred feet away, in the Salt Lake temple, nearly every day of the week, men wear that same habit of white, as do the women. Yet, out in the world of practicing Mormon "religion" it is black or dark suits and shoes. Here this day in the tabernacle, black was in vogue.

Another oddity is that in the same temple just a few hundred feet away, five days a week; several times a day; an actor, portraying Satan, is dressed in black as the cloak of a minister of "religion." This is particularly noticeable when everyone else, dozens and dozens, wear white!

My use of white as a symbol of peace was perverted that day and ridiculed. Rumors are spread even to this time that I ran around the tabernacle in a white sheet! In my closet today hangs that suit used twenty five years ago. I don't think I could fit into it anymore though without a lot of weight reduction.

I gently tested the large oak doors on the south side of the building. No sooner had I done so than the door was pushed open by an usher. I had not expected that and so we entered. Marion and John followed me into what was a darkened contrast from the outside. I made a turn to the left and began to ascend steps which I thought would lead to the podium. Part way up I realized my error, and turned around. Again, Marion and John followed suit.

Back on the main floor of the tabernacle, I proceeded to cross toward the center. I had not gone far when a number of security guards emerged from the sides of the aisle. One of them thrust his arm out to block my approach. I pushed his arm away and said, "Get out of my way, you cannot stop the work of the Lord." That statement would later become perverted to a variety of statements such as, "You cannot stop me I'm the Lord." It would be in the interests of church employees to foster such distortions.

At that moment, two burly security guards on each side grabbed me under the arms, literally lifting me off the floor carrying me backwards exactly as I had envisioned earlier, in the non-Successful approach. Other security personnel spun John around using his face to push open that large oak door through which we had moments earlier been allowed to enter. Marion was also handled by other security personnel being carried backwards out through those same doors. I was the last to be taken out backwards to the grounds of Temple Square.

Once outside, we were told we were under arrest. I asked what for and was told for trespass. "Trespass, I exclaimed. I am a beneficial owner of these premises!" I was soon to learn that no member of the church has any vested rights by which they may go upon the properties of the church without the sanction of the leaders of the church. How naïve I had been. All those years of work, support, mission, and tithes that I had paid into the church had not purchased any rights to church property.*

[* When the church was first organized and for the first 100 years, all property of the church was held in trust by the president of the church as trustee-in-trust for the beneficial use of the members. This century it was converted to a corporate sole status without the consent of church members. In that status, all property is owned by the president to do with as he wills.]

At that moment, I had a glimpse of the next step to take. As we were being led off the Temple grounds towards the West gate, Marion said, "Its okay we are still okay!" He, himself had a spiritual glimpse of the moment. I acknowledged his comment and said, "We are going into this room ". It was the booth occupied by church security personnel just inside the gate. Thereupon, I went into the booth dragging the officers and everyone inside.

Once inside, I demanded the presence of the chief of church security. This brother had been in the military and was in fact an officer in the Utah National Guard. I had seen his picture in church publications as he often traveled with the church president. He was rather short around 5'-8" or so.

The officers summoned him and he shortly appeared. His name was J. Earl Jones. I addressed him by name and told him that he knew me. "I don't know you Brother Wallace", was his response. I looked at him again and he realized he had tripped himself up. I told him that the confrontation that morning would not have been necessary had the church leaders agreed to have met with me over the past several years.

I told him my purpose could be served that day if a meeting was arranged with a member of the Council of the Twelve. He left the security booth returning about fifteen minutes later. He informed me that Elder Ashton would meet with me in the church tower at 2:30 that afternoon. He also told me that we were no longer under arrest but that we had to leave Temple Square.

Accepting the appointment to meet, I led my small group off the grounds going out through the west gate. Once outside the media were all over us. Television cameras were whirling as well as flash cameras. Questions from reporters were answered with brevity. They had asked us our names. Marion and I gave ours but John said he preferred not to. Later John was identified as Darrell Lee, my former law associate. This mistaken identity was published widely in the media resulting in Darrell filing a lawsuit against the church, Salt Lake City P. D. Associated Press and several newspapers. That lawsuit was settled out of court with Darrell receiving an amount, not published*.

The record was sealed so the world does not know the amount of settlement nor which of the defendants contributed the lion's share. Before settlement, Darrell asked me what I thought it would be worth to him and I indicated an amount. He agreed that was his thinking. He has never told me the exact amount nor have I asked.

[The reader will recall that I told Darrell in January 1974, that he would make some money from his association with me in connection with my struggles against Mormonism.]

Later Darrell would pay the price for that legal assault on the church by personal discredit which would be heaped upon him. Again the church, or rather its secret entrenched Danites, have to discredit any person who appears to have won the upper hand in a public confrontation with the church. The church has to always appear to be pure and clean at any cost to the lives of others. Similar discredit of John Evans was also orchestrated.

Outside of the West gate, I did open my black loose-leaf folder and show to television cameras copies of correspondence with church leaders to demonstrate that this was not a sudden event but had been brewing for years. To the best of my knowledge, none of that was ever shown to the public in Salt Lake or anywhere.

After talking to the media, we walked north, then east to the North gate of Temple Square. I remembered Sharon Wright was still in the Tabernacle. I led my party, which now included Darlene back onto the grounds where I ran into Detective Stoner of the S.L.C.P.D. He ordered us off the grounds again under threat of arrest for trespassing. I looked him squarely in the eyes and told him we would not leave until one of our party had been brought out of the Tabernacle.

A year later, Detective Stoner would be involved in a strong arming of the Air Marshall's office in Seattle as well as United Airlines personnel which I will detail later.

One of the church security men then used his BEE lapel pin as a microphone and instructed those inside to locate Sharon and bring her out.

As soon as Sharon rejoined our group, we walked along North Temple Street to where Darlene had parked the van. We were kept under police surveillance as we walked and we could hear police radio conversations about having located a van with Washington license plates on it. Leaving Salt Lake City, we drove north to Ogden and were followed by the police long after we had left city limits.

We returned to the motel, but first I wanted to take my party to the old Lincoln Grade school grounds where I had been earlier that morning. I wanted to see if anyone could feel anything special about that site. No one did except Sharon but I ascribed that to suggestion. The church conference was being broadcast on the radio so we listened to it. I remember Ezra Taft Benson orating on the need to shed blood in the "saving" of the U. S. Constitution. The reader will recall the delusion of Mormon Priesthood that they have a duty to "save" it.

Back at the motel, we rested until it was time to leave to go back to Salt Lake City for the interview with Elder Ashton. Elder Ashton was a member of the Twelve Apostles of the church and I was now looking forward to discussing the issue of black priesthood with him.

Upon arriving at the church tower at 50 East North Temple, I led my group to the receptionist. She made a telephone call and asked us to wait. Soon, two members of church security arrived to lead us up the elevator to I believe the sixteenth floor. These men were wearing the BEE lapel pin. Sharon made a comment about their lapel pins. They took us through a series of electronically locked doors to what could only be described as an

interrogation room. It was an inside room with no outside view. We were told Elder Ashton would be there shortly.

These men proceeded to ask questions in a purely inquisitorial fashion. A knock on the door indicated Elder Ashton was present in an adjoining room for the interview. I was told I could go in that room but my group could not. I indicated to them that it was all right and proceeded on my own. I was told later that the two security men continued to ask questions of my group during the time I was with Ashton.

Upon entering the room where Ashton was seated, I discovered I had been had by church security. The Elder Ashton I was talking to was not the Apostle Ashton but rather the head of the church Public Communication's Department. The boss, if you will, of the elder who had tried to take over the microphone at the Travelodge Motel four days earlier.

This brother Ashton was also wearing the BEE lapel pin and had not brought with him any note paper or pen to write down information he might glean from me. Instead, he, along with the other two, merely relied on all conversations being recorded elsewhere in the complex. As you can imagine, the meeting was fruitless. It ended upon my commenting that the church was like a stagnant pond in that it allowed no input from members to freshen up the water. I expressed regret for that condition. Ashton looked as if he could not comprehend my statement. Of course, Mormon priesthood arrogance was in strong display that day by those three men.

After leaving the building, we traveled to the Salt Lake Airport where John boarded a plane for Portland, as he had a work assignment the next morning. We picked up Larry Lester whom I had arranged to fly to SLC in case I had been successful in presenting the black priesthood issue. I wanted to present him to the church leaders.

Taking Larry on a tour, he pointed at the Tabernacle and exclaimed that was the steamboat shaped building in which he

had seen the leadership of the church thrown out of office. That has not yet happened but hopefully will yet one day.

That afternoon we began our return trip to Portland arriving there the next day. We did pick up newspapers en-route which had headlines about our experience in Salt Lake City and a wrong identification of John Evans as Darrell Lee.

I learned on that trip that church leaders hide behind a brick wall of armed support. They need not speak because there are literally hundreds of programmed "elders" to speak for them and defend them. I also got the impression that many of those armed men were not of the Mormon faith.

I learned that my mission was going to be much tougher that I thought. Although the Lord would prepare the way, I had to put my body in the right place for things to happen. I also learned that carefully and cautiously following dreams or precognition was the only way I could put my body in the right place at the right time. It was a factor of supreme security.

I estimated the security force at the Tabernacle to be in the hundreds. This was the beginning of an awakening for me, and soon I would be looking at facts and reading materials considered to be "anti-Mormon", which I had never allowed myself to do before this time. My education from the research of others God called to that task was now commencing which He had informed me of on the Lincoln Grade School grounds 38 years earlier.

From the Salem Oregon Statesman Newspaper April 7, 1976 Showing Marion Wright, John Evans and the Author outside the West Gate of Temple Square after being evicted from the Tabernacle talking to media people. John was miss-identified as Darrel Lee. For those who claimed the author ran around in a white sheet it is evident that a white Panama suit and white tie was his attire.

Chapter Twenty Four

Excommunication!

The evening of the day following our return from Salt Lake, we gathered at Darlene's and my home to tape record our impressions of the events of April 6th, 1976 in Salt Lake City. While we were thus assembled around the dining room table, the front door bell rang. I answered the door to find brother Roy King with a letter of summons of my person to High Council court* of the church to try me for my membership in the church. The trial date was set for Sunday April 11th. Returning to the group, we finished taping our impressions of the 6th.

[* Being a High Priest in the church, a Bishop's court had no authority]

At the press conference on the day of the ordination of Larry, I had told the media that the church could not summarily excommunicate me. They would have to follow printed church rules as established in the priesthood handbook. The rules provided for the use of a tape recorder should the defendant want to record the proceedings. Accordingly, I took a tape recorder with me.

The trial was to be held in the Stake High Council room of the Stake Center in Vancouver, Washington. As I entered the building, Church "Brothers" were hiding their faces by looking at the walls of the hallways as they scurried away. I particularly noticed that conduct on the part of the area Public Communications Officer of the church who had been present at the ordination of Larry Lester.

Going directly to the assigned room, I found all of the High Council members seated in their appropriate positions around a polished table. I proceeded to plug in my tape recorder. Stake President Orson Arnold ordered it unplugged. I again plugged it in with a statement that I had a right under Priesthood Handbook rules to use the recorder. High councilman Ed Poyfair** backed up the disconnecting of the recorder by saying," President Arnold, this is your court you have a right to conduct it as you see fit."

**[Ed Poyfair was an attorney in Vancouver, having attended Northwestern school of Law a year behind me. On occasion, at Monthly County Bar Association luncheons, He and I would walk together across the parking lot of the Quay restaurant where the meetings were held. We knew each other to be Mormons and returned missionaries. Other than that, we had had no professional or social contact.]

Having been denied my right to tape record the proceedings; I then made a motion to dismiss the charges on the grounds that my actions were not forbidden by my church membership. I indicated that I baptized Larry Lester into the Kingdom of Heaven not the Mormon Church and that further, He was ordained a priest in the Kingdom of Heaven, not the Mormon Church and therefore the church was without jurisdiction to try me for conduct not forbidden by written rules. I attempted to chart this reality on the blackboard on the wall of the room. One of the High Councilmen erased my writing as fast as I could put it on the board.

That motion was denied, again, by the support of Ed Poyfair who may have been a civil attorney but was far short of being knowledgeable of the Priesthood Handbook at that time.

According to the handbook, six members of the council were to speak in my defense. The other six could be prosecutorial. The pivotal vote was that Of the Stake President. I witnessed no members of the council speaking in my defense; it was a stacked Kangaroo court with orders from Salt Lake to excommunicate me.

At that moment, I served papers of ecclesiastical complaint on Spencer W. Kimball, The First Presidency of the Church and the Quorum of the Twelve, as then constituted. I charged them with violating the trust of the church by converting the assets of the church to their own personal use, of creating an armed secret order within the church and of violating the civil rights of members of the church. I served these papers upon Orson

Arnold as the personal representative of the named defendants. He thrust them face down on the table.

I told him the rules of equity now required that he terminate the instant proceedings to abide the outcome of a trial in a High Priest's Court of the church to be later assembled in Salt Lake City. I told him, that my standing to bring such suit within the church was based upon my membership and that he could not now terminate that standing by excommunication. Equity and fairness demanded that he cease conducting proceedings against me until after the leaders first stood church trial.

Orson Arnold by occupation was a dental lab technician. Being confronted by the actions of an attorney, he was totally bewildered. Again Ed Poyfair attempting to act as a legal counsel to the Stake President said to me, "Brother Wallace, you know me." I responded that I did not know him since we had nothing in common. He bowed his head.

** [Ed Poyfair later became a court judge in Vancouver. I met him in an elevator in the Clark County Courthouse in late December 1996. He didn't recognize me but after introducing myself we shook hands with his comment, "I didn't think you were still around."]

At this point, I told Arnold to cancel the trial and began to leave. He ordered me to sit down. I told him I was leaving, the proceedings were over. One or two of the council members approached me with the thought of putting their hands on me to restrain me; I asked which of them wanted a lawsuit for false arrest. They then backed off and I left.

I was home less than fifteen minutes when Roy King appeared at the front door with a letter of excommunication. Obviously, there was not time for the Council to have discussed the issue. Orders came down from Salt Lake and those orders were complied with. The letter of excommunication had been prepared prior to the assembling of the "kangaroo court" Another right extended to excomunicants by the Priesthood Handbook, was a right to trial de novo by the First Presidency of the church. Appeal was taken and a trial de novo was erroneously denied.

Because of the conduct of the council in violating the written rules, I am, under equity, still a member of the church and a High Priest therein. The complaint which I filed against the church leaders has yet to be held before any validity of my alleged excommunication may be obtained. Based upon the outstanding complaint I had served, two events occurred which I will write about later.

Chapter Twenty Five

Opening the Mind

Excommunication has a very beneficial effect. First, you discover yourself among a very elite group of people. Secondly, for the first time you have the courage to look at the other side of the Mormon coin.

I can remember the days of being totally gung-ho about the Mormon Church (and also very ignorant). On the mission to England, there were times when I would be placed in a very stressful position of defending the church. My first such experience was at Hyde Park corner in London, where we missionaries would mount a soapbox and preach the "gospel" to anyone who would stop and listen. There were of course, "professional" hecklers who loved to trip up a new missionary in his or her understanding of the Mormon doctrines.

Our baptism of fire occurred the first night in London on the first day of the mission. When my turn came, I mounted the soapbox and made the mistake of quoting a not too doctrinal axiom learned early in the church relating to the notion of eternal progression. "Man is as God once was and God is as man may become," which I blurted out only to be shot down by a heckler. I was put into a very uncomfortable position with a hopeless defense.

The next day arriving in Birmingham, I was taken from the train directly to the "Bull Ring" where I experienced a repeated performance of soapbox preaching and being shot down by a heckler. After I said my mother had come from Birmingham, he called her a "whore"*. I was ready to take off my coat and go at it. The District President had to intervene to keep this green missionary from going ballistic! Many other times I would be required to rise to the defense of Mormonism.

[*belief that the practice of polygamy was still official in Utah was at the root of his statement]

However, the excommunication proceedings, in the face of a blatant disregard for printed rules, worked like a steel wedge in my cramped tight brain.

At the time of the ordination of Larry Lester, I still believed that the church was divinely organized, indeed "restored" to its original form as of the time of Christ. Without question I knew things were not then right and believed that it had strayed from the path. I believed also that my spiritual dilemma had to do with bringing the church back into line as at first. I believed in the words of the hymn written by Eliza Snow

Awake ye Saints of God awake

Call on the Lord in mighty prayer!

And bring to naught the tempter's snare.

And bring to naught the tempter's snare!

Soon I would learn that all was never right with the church. In time, I would learn that:

* Joseph Smith Jr. was an over-sexed charlatan.

* He never had a "First Vision".

* Sidney Rigdon* was likely the "Angel Moroni."as well as "John the Baptist" in the Susquehanna River.

* The Book of Mormon was a double redaction* of a book by that title written by Solomon Spalding a graduate of Dartmuth College in New Hampshire where a cousin of Joseph Smith, Jr., Ethan

Smith, also attended and wrote a book called A View of The Hebrews.

* Sidney Rigdon was the redactor and presented the Work to Joseph Smith with whom he had conspired for several years beforehand. Etc., etc., etc.

Not long after the ordination and "excommunication", I received a call from Dr. John Fitzgerald, a retired educator living in the outskirts of Salt Lake City. He had been excommunicated because he mounted a campaign of writing letters to the editor of the Salt Lake Tribune newspaper in which he attempted to intellectualize the inappropriateness of the church denying priesthood to blacks.

He wanted to meet me and suggested I visit him in Holladay, Utah. Darlene was shortly to attend a convention of the Hillhaven Corporation there and I asked her if she would make contact with John. I wanted to know what kind of person he was. She did so after preparing an oil painting which she gave John and his wife Mary*. Twenty-three years later that painting was still hanging on the wall of their living room!

Upon returning from the conference, Darlene explained That John was a delightful person and I should meet him. She brought back some materials he had given her. Among these were materials on Egyptian Papyri which Joseph Smith claimed were the original writings of father Abraham which he, Smith, claimed to have translated into the Book of Abraham as contained in a collection of Standard works of the church called the Pearl of Great Price.

The papyri were thought to have been destroyed in the Chicago fire but turned up in the early 1960's in the basement of the Metropolitan Museum in New York City. The church purchased them and asked Hugh Nibley, a BYU professor to translate them Nibley fooled around with them for some time writing abstract comments in the monthly church magazine, The Ensign. It turned out that the church also asked Mormon "professor", Dee Jay Nelson, an Egyptologist to translate them. Nelson went right to work and discovered the papyri were nothing more than a funeral commentary of a man named HOR. There was not one lick of connection with the "Book of Abraham". The church refused to discuss the truth with Nelson, but allowed Nibley to continue his ramblings. Nelson, his wife and daughter resigned from the church and today, the church continues to support the lie that the Book of Abraham came from those papyri!

Little by little I learned that Mormonism was a fraud from day one. I became despaired that the leaders knew of the fraud and lies for which many faithful saints had given their all, including their lives, to place these deceivers into a perpetual prestigious power position over them.

I met many other persons with whom I could intelligently communicate. Most of these had challenged the doctrines and practices of the church only to find themselves cast out by excommunication. Indeed this association I found myself in was a holy association. I was learning anew the real history of the Mormon Church. These people were among those whom had been called to research the truth which I was to one day use to defeat the Mormon leaders.

Chapter Twenty Six

Visions of Tomorrow Year

Between April 1976 and July 1978 I was the recipient of numerous dreams and precognition concerning the future of my struggles to expose the fraud and corruption of Mormonism. I did not write these down at the time with one exception. I will attempt to relate them from memory in somewhat the order they came.

Around the first week of May 1976 I lay awake in bed after having gone through what Darlene said was several days of being "out of it". By that she meant I had spent a lot of time in total concentration of what I guess could be called the spirit. I was now waiting for Darlene to wake up. When she did, I told her that I was going tell her a bunch of things which I wanted her to write down. I also said to her that she was going to tell me she didn't need to as she could remember them. She then said she didn't need to write them down as she could remember them. Realizing I had said that would be her response, she got up and brought a yellow pad back to bed.

I proceeded to take a shower and returned to bed. Darlene was just finishing up her writing. I asked her about the various things I had said to see if she had written them down. I had to remind her of only a few items. It then became time to find a place to place the document so that they would be preserved. She went to her dresser and placed it in the top drawer. I reminded her that her daughters often got into that drawer to take out items of clothing of hers to wear. Did she want them to see the document? She recovered the document and came back to bed to ponder where she should place it. She then got up and placed it in a situation which neither of us can remember.

At the time, I recall telling her that was very good but would we remember where? I told her to go ahead: if the Lord wanted us to find it we would. Even though there have been many changes in our lives including divorce, we have not been able to locate that document to this date.

Mt. St Helens

During the dictation of those future events, I mentioned That when some of the events would happen, Mt St. Helens in Southwest Washington State will have lost it's "cone". By that I meant the very top of the mountain would be gone. Darlene commented that the snow cone is gone every year. I told her not just the snow but the mountain itself. I would remind the reader that on May 19th of 1980, four full years later, a volcanic eruption occurred in which the mountain lost its cone.

A Red Brick Building at Night

I saw two men talking. These men wore civilian clothes but appeared to be either security personnel or undercover police. They were in two separate vehicles but were parked in different directions each looking and talking to the other through open driver's door windows.

It was night time. They were on surveillance, observing the exterior of a large red brick building. From a head-on position across the street. A large lighted breezeway was at the center main floor of the two storied building, a discussion of an occupant of the building was held. One of these men pulled out his hand gun gesturing with it pointing it at the lighted breezeway he said," If that S.O.B. came out of that door right now, I would blow his F-----g brains out". Simultaneously, he swung his weapon toward the head of the other man and instinctively pulled the trigger resulting in a shot being fired at the back of the neck.

A Prison Break

I saw a crowded bar or nightclub scene. Seated at a table was a well dressed man in a dark suit. He appeared to have the manners and arrogance of either an FBI agent or a Mormon. Seated across the table from him, was a man in clean but casual clothes. A discussion was being held concerning a possible prison break.

I saw the man in the suit give a quantity of currency to the other man. The words, "All you have to do is turn your back and not look," were said..

Next I saw two galvanized pipes made up in a hook shape go down over razor wire on the top of what appeared to be a prison wall. I saw inmates in prison garb scampering over the wall then dropping to the ground. They ran across an open field toward some woods. Prison guards were shouting at a tower guard near the escape point but the guard had turned his back and pretended not to hear.

One of the prisoners told the others it was everyone for themselves. Except he grabbed a short, slightly built prisoner and told him to come with him. They ran toward a road looking for a culvert. Upon finding it, the first man reached into it. He pulled out a paper sack and opened it. He then took out a gun and some currency. He swore a little and pointing the gun at the other said," Bam! You're dead if you didn't know what this was all about." He gave the money to the shorter man and took the gun. They then split up.

I saw each of the prisoners captured. One under some leaves, another in a little church house.

Boise Airport Incident

From inside the airport terminal building, I saw a long black limousine pull up to the outside curb. A man in a dark suit emerged from the front passenger door and opened the rear door of the vehicle.

Then a small woman with dark hair got out. She was wearing dark glasses and a flower corsage. She was led into the building and joined by several other men in dark suits. They positioned themselves at the bottom of the escalator which led to the arrival/departure gates. Each time a plane would arrive, they would wait at the bottom of the escalator as if to greet someone.

After a long time, the public address system instructed Tricia Conner to go to the white courtesy telephone. In the dream I knew that the woman was supposed to be Tricia Conner but this woman never stirred as if she didn't know her own name.

There were several items I received but which I cannot remember and likely never will except that the document written by Darlene should surface somewhere.

Chapter Twenty Seven

Assessing the Situation

During the middle of September 1976, I drove to Salt Lake City (SLC) to meet Dr. John and Mary Fitzgerald. They lived in the Carriage Lane retirement condo complex in Holladay, Utah. John was about 70 years of age at the time. He was a retired school principal. After retirement he began to write letters to the editor of the Salt Lake Tribune giving very strong scriptural and ethical arguments against the Mormon Church continuing its ban of Black priesthood.

He was excommunicated for that activity. His wife however continued to be active in the church. She was also retired from a teaching career. After a while, tongue wagging began in which it was inferred that John had been excommunicated on moral grounds. That kind of defamation caused John to become angry. Being cut off from the church because of his intellectual honesty was acceptable to John but he could not come to terms with his character being disparaged.

In the condo complex, John and his wife had a two-bedroom apartment. It was in a two story, eight-unit building. Their apartment was on the first floor. The front door opened into a two-story breezeway.

Across the campus in the basement of an adjoining building, John had made his allocated storage unit into an office/den where he could retire for the day engaging in intellectual pursuits. Chief among those pursuits was writing letters to the editor.

In addition, he wrote poems which he privately published. Books on other subjects were also privately bound. One of these was titled "Discrimination: Is if of God?" He and two other individuals co-authored that book. I was the recipient of a copy on my first visit.

John introduced me to several individuals who had broken away from the stereotype Mormons. Among these were Jerald and Sandra Tanner. The Tanners had written a book, MOMONISM: SHADOW OR REALITY. The book was pretty much filled with microfilm copies of early church documents. Reading what the early Mormon leaders had to say about the various facets of the "gospel" leads one to recognize the fatal flaws in Mormonism.

Another individual was Michael Marquardt who had co-authored the Discrimination book with John. It was a good feeling to be able to openly discuss the pros and cons of Mormonism with intelligent people who had the courage to stray from the spoon-fed path and take a hard look at the other side of Mormonism.

The purpose for the trip to Utah at this time had to do with my making an assessment about what I was going to do next. There was no mistaking the hand of God in bringing together the situations and events which led to the ordination of Larry Lester. However, I was at a stalemate to know what I should now do to keep the mission alive. Because of that, I was very attentive to the visit I was now making.

Many hours were spent discussing these matters with John. I was at times humored by his dry wit. I can remember one of his quotes: "Nothing is absolute including that statement!" For the next two years I was a welcome guest in the home of John and Mary whenever circumstances led me to Utah.

On the way back to Vancouver, I had the notion that I must get some kind of an organization together. In January of that year, when Roy King came into my home trying to discover my organization and supporters, I had no organization. By the time of the ordination, I had a very select few to walk with me, but since that time I was pretty much winging it alone.

Occasionally, something would come up so that the media would contact me for an interview, but for the most part I was stalemated.

It dawned on me to organize a non-profit entity which I would call The LDS Freedom Foundation. The intent and purpose was to hopefully align myself with others who had come to an understanding that Mormonism was a fraud and completely different from what had been taught to us as children. In doing so, I intended to print a periodical. I also hoped to raise a little funding to assist me in my endeavors.

Arriving home, I proceeded to incorporate the LDS Freedom Foundation, adopting the Dexter arm of the Wallace coat of arms as a symbol to be placed on a letterhead. It is raised with sword and the accompanying motto pro libertate (for liberty). I cut and pasted the letterhead using the self-stick letters then available.

Using that letter head, I wrote a letter to Spencer W. Kimball indicating I would proceed to hold ecclesiastical trial on the brethren pursuant to the complaint I had served upon Orson Arnold at the proceedings for excommunication last April 11th. I indicated the trial would take place at the Tabernacle during the October semi-annual conference of the church. I also declared that the opportunity would never again be available for his security personnel to put their hands on me as they did on April 6th

In a sense I was bluffing for reality told me that I was powerless in myself to prevent such a thing. However, being prompted by the spirit to do so, I would let God take care of that situation and, I should add, God did! I knew that I would not again recklessly place myself in that position as I had at April Conference. With spiritual assurance, I would be safe each step of the way. Without it, I would hesitate going forward. I was dealing with armed security personnel in the tradition of gunslinger Orrin Porter Rockwell. He was the notorious bodyguard of Joseph Smith, Jr. and Brigham Young. As such, he was founder of Church security. For that reason, discretion would be the better part of valor. The letter was sent and I waited on the Lord.

Dr. John Fitzgerald a very courageous man

John Passed away in late 1998

Chapter Twenty Eight

The Legal Engagement

Two or three days before October Semi-annual Conference, I received a telephone call from Dave Briscoe of the Associated Press office in SLC. He wanted to know what I was going to do about the temporary restraining order (TRO). "What?" I asked. It appeared that the church had gone into Third District (State) Court in SLC and obtained a TRO to keep me off Temple Square during the conference. I told Dave I would check it out and let him know.

I called the Utah Bar Association to obtain a referral attorney to assist me. They gave me the name of Brian Barnard. The attorney who gave me that referral acknowledged he was a Mormon but I had every right to a defense attorney. I called Brian and made arrangements to meet him at the West Gate of Temple Square on Sunday at 1:00 PM.

I called John Fitzgerald and he said he would pick me up at the airport. The next morning I received a copy of the TRO in the mail from Oscar McKonkie a church attorney. The cover letter admonished me to "conduct myself accordingly". What Oscar didn't understand was that I had been conducting myself according to instructions from the Lord given to me in dreams and precognition. Unfortunately, that conduct came into conflict with the church. Putting my trust in God was the only thing I could do under the circumstances.

John met me at the airport and drove me over to Temple Square. The scene there was an ordinary lazy kind of in-between conference sessions break on a sunny Sunday afternoon. I met Brian Barnard. He was a tall sturdily built man with a very soft voice. He wore his hair in a ponytail. I instantly liked him.

No church security personnel were present at the gate to prevent my entrance had I wished to walk on in. Indeed, had I

170

"conducted" myself in a low profile manner, no one would have likely even known I was present. That was not the purpose for the visit however. I had been instructed to "engage" the church and that I would do. The copy of the TRO sent to me by McKonkie was not sufficient in law to bind me to the restraints of the order. I had to be actually and personally served by someone who could execute an affidavit that I had been served. Oscar must have assumed that I would be frightened off by the order as no steps appeared to have been taken to personally serve me.

I entered the west gate going directly to the same security booth into which I had dragged all those men the previous April conference. I spoke to a woman in there telling her my name and that there was supposed to be a restraining order to be served upon me. Did she have a copy or did they want to have someone else serve me.

After a telephone call or so a security person appeared and told me that a deputy sheriff would be over in a few minutes to serve me would I please wait outside of the grounds? I complied and about twenty minutes later the deputy arrived with the order and served it upon me.

By this time the media had gotten word I was at the gate and they began to assemble and to video tape the event. I was asked why, being an attorney myself, did I retain Brian as my attorney. I explained that it was an arrangement of his being co-counsel. I also explained that the church had violated law in the manner in which they had obtained the TRO. Under law, the plaintiff must make at least a minimal effort to notify the defendant that they were going to court to obtain such an order. The rule is designed to provide the defendant an opportunity to argue against the sought order.

Over the next few months, I was to learn that the Mormon Church is not required to meet those standards of conduct by the Utah courts. In this matter, the church had not sought to inform

me and the court never questioned that deficiency. For that reason I argued it was necessary for me to have local counsel to prevent that kind of thing from happening again. Since we were going to engage the church in legal combat, it was also very important that local court rules be timely complied with. I lived a long way away from the Utah court and Brian provided me that protection.

Brian addressed the media explaining that the conduct of the church in obtaining the TRO had violated my First Amendment right to the free exercise of religion and that we would counter-sue the church for damages.

As I was discussing my position regarding the black priesthood issue, I observed a man of about 35 years of age circling around the group becoming increasingly agitated. I spoke to him and asked him what the matter was. He responded that I was the matter. I was offending the church president and God by my conduct. I responded that if he really felt that way perhaps he should pray about it.

"Will you kneel here on this sidewalk and pray with me," he asked. I said, "Sure." In his offering, he told God to straighten me out and get me back into compliance with church order. Afterwards we shook hands and I asked him if he believed God would answer his prayer to which he responded, "You know He will!" I then asked him what it would mean if God's answer was that I keep doing what I was. His eyes glazed over and he walked away considering that question but at least now calmed from his anxiety. Six months later he would apologize for that behavior.

Brian had obtained a copy of the TRO from the court clerk's office and had prepared a counter suit that he was able to file early the following week. I spent a few days with John and Mary and then returned home.

The conduct restrained by a TRO is temporary only and must be converted to an injunction if it is to be permanently restrained.

The October '76 order expired by law some 20 days after it was issued. Therefore I was no longer restrained by the order during the pending of a court hearing on the merits of the complaint for injunction. We were bogged down in court and no full trial date had been set. During that period, some motions were heard. One of the causes of action we had filed was dismissed by the court and we appealed it before trial on the other issues.

The Utah Supreme Court rendered a decision on that appeal before the actual trial began so that it was a matter of record at the time of trial. The court ruled for the church which is to be expected in the political arena of Utah. However, the court in doing so made use of allegations made against me by church security personnel that I had said, "Don't touch me I am the Lord!" The court used that statement as a finding of fact when indeed it had never been ruled such in the trial court simply because the trial had not yet been had!

Later it was easy to use that statement against my character as a fact simply because the Utah Supreme Court had ruled it so! Later when arguments on appeal of the lower court ruling after trial were had, one of the Justices asked me why I served notice of prejudice upon all justices of the court. The answer was easy. They had demonstrated that prejudice in the prior ruling!

While those skirmishes were going on, The 1977 April Conference of the church was approaching. I engaged in a lot of meditation. I wrote another letter to Spencer W. Kimball stating that since there was not a TRO preventing it, I would proceed with the promised trial of church leaders at April conference. I prepared an agenda and timetable for that trial which I included. Again, I waited upon the Lord.

By March of 1977, I was involved in some construction work in Shelton, Washington. Sharon Wright had introduced me to Don Benson, a real estate broker who went by the business name of Benson Realty. The work consisted of remodeling the interior of what had been a large plumber's shop building. The purpose being to construct several office suites within it. One of these

would be a new office for Benson Realty. In fact it was the first office suite completed.

While finishing that office, I received another telephone call from Dave Briscoe of the Associated Press office in SLC. Had I heard the church obtained another TRO to prevent my attendance at the April conference? It was Friday and the order was effective for that weekend. I called Brian but he had not heard anything about it. The church had again violated civil law by not notifying Brian or myself prior to going to court. The court had also again shown its bias toward the church by not insisting on such required notice

A reservation was made for my flight on United Airlines Saturday morning. At the gate, I waited for everyone to board the plane so that I could observe what was happening. Finally, they issued the final boarding call. A well dressed man in a black suit was hanging around the gate attendant's desk. I didn't know if he was going to board or not. I waited for a minute and he did not appear to respond to the call. I decided then to board.

As I walked down the aisle to about midway of the craft I caught the eye of someone I recognized but couldn't place. I later learned it was detective Stoner of the Salt Lake City Police Department who had arrested and un-arrested me on Temple Square a year earlier.

My seat was about two seats behind him on the right or seat C on the aisle. No sooner did I sit down than that man got up and walked into the flight deck cabin where he remained all the way to SLC.

Shortly, the dark suited man* who had been waiting at the gate, boarded the plane. He walked past me and talked with another man** seated behind me. After a few minutes he got off the plane.

*[*This individual was later confronted by Channel 2 reporter, Dean Jones. He had an office in the Equitable building in Portland with no name on the door. According to Jones this individual had a concealed weapon permit and was very ruffled when Jones knocked on his door.*

he would not let Jones and his cameraman into the office. He stood in the doorway; as he explained he was having an affair with a woman in Boise intending to go there to see her but after boarding the plane decided his wife might find out and therefore he got off. That of course does not square, with what actually happened on the plane. The guy was clearly a member of the Mormon Mafia also known as Danites. The armed enforcers of the Mormon conspiracy. I later filed a federal lawsuit for damages over this conspiracy and learned that Stoner and his partner had gone to Seattle and strong-armed both United Airlines Security and the Federal Air Marshal's Office to be allowed to travel on the flight with guns in violation of law.]

[**That man was another SLCPD detective and the partner of Stoner]

Instead of doing a push off for departure, it was announced that all passengers boarding in Portland would have to leave the plane to have their luggage searched in the Customs shed.

I and the others got off the plane and went to Customs where our luggage was searched. When I got back on the plane, a woman seated next to me asked what was all that about? I jokingly said maybe they are looking for a bomb*.

[*Little did I know at the time allegations had been made that I would be taking explosives to Utah! It later turned out that the military bomb disposal squad from Hill Air Force Base had been sent to the Tabernacle for the occasion.]

About 45 minutes of delay in departure from Portland had occurred. Finally, we were off and on our way to Salt Lake City with a stop over at Boise, Idaho after which, the plane landed in Salt Lake City. There were no second floor gates and ramps connecting to the plane at the terminal building. Passengers descended stairs walking across the tarmac toward the building. As I approached the glass doors, several blinding lights from television cameras flashed on.

A few feet inside the entrance, I was met by a uniformed deputy of the Salt Lake County sheriff's office. He asked my name and handed me a copy of the second illegally obtained TRO.

Media reporters were present asking questions. I said very little but was met by John Fitzgerald who described what he had observed in preparation for my arrival. John drove a very small Subaru car and his reactions were not too fast. In fact, I felt anxiety in the middle of intersections when he came nearly to a complete stop to decide which way he wanted to turn. Unknown by us at the time, we were being tailed by city cops.

John drove to his friend LaMar Peterson's home first where I was introduced to LaMar and his wife. Both of them had been excommunicated from the church because of LaMar's writings questioning the authenticity of church history. LaMar wanted to thank me on behalf of intellectuals within the church for my having taken my stand on Black priesthood.

Later at John's condo, Mary had prepared a meal. After watching the evening news with videos of my arrival at the airport, we retired to bed. I slept in the den in which a twin size bed had been placed under the window. I slept for about three hours and then awoke. As I lay there pondering what I would do at Temple Square in the morning, a very loud, sharp pistol shot rang out! My first thoughts were of domestic violence in the complex. I thought of rushing out to offer help. But where would I go? What direction?

Realizing that I could do nothing in the dark I lay there hoping no one was hurt.

Less than five minutes later, flashing red lights rotated on the window drapes. An emergency vehicle had gone past. No siren was heard it was a silent code 3. I heard no more. Believing appropriate emergency personnel had answered a call to what ever had happened, I later fell asleep.

At the breakfast table, I asked John and Mary if they had heard anything during the night....like a gunshot. They hadn't. The Sunday morning newspaper, The Salt Lake Tribune, had a headline: Salt Lake Police Officer Accidentally Shot in East County. I asked John where exactly was east county? His response was, "Here--right here in Holladay!"

It had been arranged for me to meet Brian at the West Gate to Temple Square at 10:00 A.M... He had prepared a summons to be served upon church president Spencer W. Kimball. I asked John to park some three or so blocks west of the temple grounds. This I did based upon déjà vu I was having as we drove into the area. We got out and walked a zigzag pattern to arrive at the west gate. Something told me to not put myself in line of fire* from the rooftop of the Hotel Utah.

*[*Eleven years later, a report was read to me over the telephone that snipers been atop the hotel with orders to shoot me.]*

The media were present at the gate as well as a number of church security personnel. Brian asked one of them to bring church attorney Wilford Kirten* to the gate for purposes of serving papers upon him.

*[*Kirten was the church attorney who delivered the Dummar, "Hughes Will" to the probate Court in Las Vegas]*

A few minutes later Kirten appeared. I served the summons for Spencer Kimball upon him. The media took pictures of that service which were published the next morning. After some 45 minutes, John and I left returning to his home.

Next morning I had an appointment with Brian at his office. Since I knew he had rapport with personnel at the police station just across the street, I asked him if he would check on the shooting of the previous morning.

I was recalling the dream of a year earlier. I wanted to find out if what had happened was what I had seen. If it were, I would be able to expose the truth about the accident. Brian was gone for about a half hour. When he returned he gave me the address of the shooting. The address, on Kayland Way was immediately across Holladay Blvd. from John and Mary's condo. In fact, it was the intersection you looked at as you left the breezeway of their 8-unit building. Brian also questioned why these officers in civilian clothing were in privately owned vans on a police surveillance matter.

It all came clear to me. I asked Brian to set up a press conference at the west gate of Temple Square for 4:00 P.M... I would expose the truth of the shooting! On the way home, I told John to drive to the intersection of Kayland and turn right. I then asked him to slow down and look out of his window to see blood on the pavement. He was excited; he said "Yes, I can see it." We stopped and I took pictures. Across Holladay Blvd. stood the red brick 8-unit building which contained John and Mary's condo. It was exactly as I had seen in the series of dreams a year earlier!

At 4:00 P. M John and I along with Brian, were present at the west gate where I held a press conference. Up to that time, the police had been evasive to reporter's inquiries about the accidental shooting. For the press conference, I had drawn a map showing the location of the shooting in proximity to John's condo. I told those assembled that officer Olson was shot while holding sack on me.

When the news hit the television stations that evening and the papers in the morning, there was a lot of squirming on the part of the police. At first the new police chief denied any connection but was forced later to admit it was true.

A few days following that incident, the motion calendar was heard in Third District court. Our motion for trial setting came up. I stood up making reference to the shooting of officer Olson and demanded that a trial date be set to avoid any further accidents such as had happened. The court set trial for the middle of August.

Outside of the Court House, a small group of my supporters had assembled. They wanted to meet to see how they could raise some money to help me with expenses. I noticed a petite Hispanic looking woman in the group. At a nearby restaurant we were seated around a large table when John told the assembled group about his experience with me as I had directed him to the blood on the street pavement on Kayland Way.

I spoke up and said that I didn't know how it happened but that I have periods of precognition in which I see events and then Deja vu when the event actually happens. I mentioned that was the case as we then all sat around the table. Suddenly the little Hispanic gal had a headache! Her name was Tricia Conner. One of the ladies said she had some aspirin in her purse but Tricia rejected it and left in a hurry.

The next day in Brian's office two detectives we knew wanted to speak to Brian and me. They said that the previous day they had noticed Tricia Conner in our group and they wanted to let me know that she used to work for SLCPD intelligence but she had been fired for her communist connections. They didn't want me to think she still worked for them in case I learned of her former employment, and would suspect she was a plant.

I was way ahead of them in the matter and the truth was that she still worked for police intelligence having infiltrated my group on behalf of Ezra Taft Benson of the church. She would later play a role in the Boise airport incident.

During the week following the shooting, Brian attended press conferences at the police station. The city had a new police chief and he had stated there was no connection between the accidental shooting of Officer Olson and Me. Later the truth was forced out and he admitted the connection. However, the church attempted to distance itself from the matter saying the surveillance was a police matter* and the church was not involved. Yet in time it became apparent it was church security that had triggered the situation with false assertions I would have explosives with me.

[* Officer Olson was alleged to have committed suicide about three years later. He had been paralyzed from the neck down by the accident. His "suicide" came after he had written a letter to the editor of the Salt Lake Tribune in which he said that church president Spencer

W. Kimball ought to be in his wheelchair if he continues to insist the church had nothing to do with the stake out of Doug Wallace.]

179

Another event which happened the week following the shooting was the re-appearance of Ken Pangborn. Ken you recall had been the fellow who was agitated at the west gate to Temple Square at the October conference. I had been asked to appear at a radio talk show to answer questions of listeners. While on the air I could see Ken through the glass partitions. During a commercial break, I went out to speak with him.

He wanted me to know that he was sorry for his behavior six months earlier. He felt that some how his agitation had hastened the accidental shooting of Olson. I told him there could be no connection whatever. He reassured me that he still believed Spencer Kimball to be a prophet of God. However, he did not think that the true church of God needed to have an armed intelligence unit.

I asked him to explain. Apparently as he attempted to approach me the past Sunday at the corner of West Temple and South Temple streets he was apprehended by an individual who refused him passage up the street. He said the man was church intelligence. Ken had properly asked by what authority this man refused him the right to walk up a public sidewalk.

Reaching into his suit pocket, the individual produced a business card, which had imprinted on it "Church Intelligence". As the man did this, Ken said he saw a large capacity automatic handgun in a shoulder holster.

Ken left the station after that. I never saw him again.

Officer Olson

Salt Lake City vice-squad Officer David Olson Was "accidentally" shot in the back of the neck by fellow Officer Michael B. Roberts while staked out watching the John Fitzgerald residence in which the Author was staying during the April 1977 Church Conference. Author had seen the event in a dream 1 year before.

Scene of Olson shooting early Sunday morning of The April 1977 Conference at corner of Holladay Blvd. and Kay land Way The Fitzgerald's condo where Author was staying was just across Holladay Blvd.

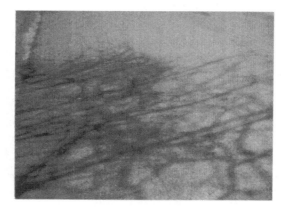

Officer Olson's blood from shooting still on pavement of Kayland Way next day after shooting. Authorities had failed to clean it off. This allowed the Author to direct Dr. Fitzgerald to the sight to confirm his previous dream of the event. At a meeting of Doug's supporters this confirmation by John caused police undercover agent Tricia Conner to leave abruptly with a head ache.

Foot Note to Chapter: Some readers may question why the author wished to respond to the church's legal assault. The church had filed a lawsuit to prevent him from an exercise of his First Amendment rights. The purpose then of the author in taking up the legal gauntlet was to lock the church in a court ruling that would establish a future legal right to do an ecclesiastical trial of the "Brethren" on temple square.

That right was established after trial by court ruling (order). In this case it is now a matter of right confirmed by the Utah Supreme Court. (page200 infra)

The "Brethren" will yet be thrown out of office as seen in Larry Lester's dream of a steamboat shaped building (page152supra) as well as Betty Moretti's and author's own precognition!

Chapter Twenty Nine

Darlene's Ordeal Begins

A number of significant events happened between October of 1976 and October of 1977. I will attempt to detail these happenings in order. At the time of the ordination of Larry Lester, Darlene was the administrator for the Hillhaven nursing home in Vancouver Washington. Some time after that the Hillhaven Corporation made some acquisitions of property, which needed upgrading. One of these was located in the hospital area of northwest Portland Oregon. Darlene was transferred to that facility.

Darlene's method of administration was never rooted in the fear pyramid. She was genuinely concerned about her patients and her staff. She managed to balance those concerns with the corporate profit incentive. Even if she had to discharge an employee out of concern for the profit factor, it was done with love and concern for the welfare of the employee.

It was no secret that my activities in pursuing my religious objectives did not allow for very much of a financial contribution to our home. What I personally earned at this time financed my travel and my efforts. In the spring of 1977, a friend of mine who had been a reporter for the Columbian Newspaper in Vancouver was now a reporter for the Seattle Post-Intelligencer. I had handled an adoption of a Korean daughter for him and his wife when I had earlier practiced law in Woodland.

In July 1977, Jack Hopkins wrote an article about my efforts, which pretty much stated my wife was the primary breadwinner for the family. About the same time, Darlene and I attended a social for the Oregon Nursing home Association at its annual gathering. I was introduced to the president of the association whom I learned was a Mormon.

At that meeting, this fellow told me as much about myself as I knew. Later he attempted to hire Darlene as his assistant. That effort went on for some time. I was concerned the church would have access to information and influence because of that relationship. I suggested to Darlene that she make salary demands an unjustifiable high level and that they be non-negotiable. Ultimately he gave up on that effort.

Later, about September or early October, The Oregon State licensing agency for nursing homes got into the act. They placed an investigator in the facility for a continuous survey looking for any defect by which the license of the facility could be jeopardized.

Having an investigator in the facility for such a long period of time put everyone under stress. Finally, the investigator was walking down a hallway past an open door to a two bed ward only to see a nurse taking a bandage off a patient then folding it over and placing it on the cover of the adjacent unoccupied bed. Obviously, this isolated incident had not been observed in the previous six weeks.

Within minutes, a notice of non-compliance with infection control was served upon Darlene. All efforts to dissuade the state from shutting down the facility were in vain. Finally, in November Darlene resigned.

For some strange reason, that resignation resolved the "out of infection control" complaint of the state. Indeed, it appeared that the state or at least one or more of its agents was hell bent on destroying Darlene's credentials so that she would be black listed and unemployable as an administrator. Indeed, it was many years before Darlene was able to restore those credentials.

Nevertheless she had established her reputation as an effective administrator in a skilled nursing facility and was sought as a roving investigator and troubleshooter by nursing home owners for several years afterwards. In writing this chapter, I sent the above material to Darlene for review and she responded as follows.

"In response to your book: Also while employed with Hillhaven, the surveyor came into the facility with a four-battery large flash light and while on rounds with the DNS looked at all 135 residents perineum and had the DNS pull back the foreskin on male patients to see if she could find any uncleanliness. I objected to this outrageous invasion of privacy and we wrote a Policy that stated the surveyor or [any] another governmental official would have to gain permission from the responsible party or a court order prior to performing any such invasive procedure of privacy violation. The surveyors were so angry they gave me a weekly survey at 4:00 PM every Friday until I resigned for the sake of the staff being so stressed out.

As you know I received a phone call every night at 11:00 PM or an early 6:30 or 7:00am phone call where no one would speak for a year. Only until I told the caller they were Satanic, did one person respond with voice to say, "It is your husband that is the cause of all this". All the other events occurred that you mentioned."

The resignation of Darlene happened in November of 1977. This was the beginning of an awful awareness on my part that her safety and well being and that of our young son hinged on a separation between us. I could not risk her life or that of our son to exposure of the assassins of the Danite order. Nor could I allow them to use the threat of harm to either of them as a weapon to control my actions.

As it happened her verbal support of my activity made her a target of the sinister side of Mormonism. In this regard it would have been better had she taken the position of neutrality, telling others that what I was doing was my thing not hers.

In Chapter 26 you will recall, I had Darlene write notes a year earlier, which included information that she would be involved in two marriages* subsequent to that of ours. Those notes were lost and we shall never be able to confirm that fact unless they someday surface.

*[*This turned out to be true. Her first subsequent marriage ended just a year or two after marriage when her husband had a massive heart attack. Several years later she married again]*

In any event, for this and other reasons, we began a partial separation within months of this experience and a complete separation in January of 1979. Divorce was not final until the summer of 1980,.

As I see it now, apart from love there were three primary reasons for the marriage. The first was that Darlene provided a safe environment for raising my son of the prior marriage. Second was the creating of our son who is today far beyond his years in judgment and maturity. Thirdly, she became a witness for the truth of the prophetic nature of the dream/precognitions I experienced during the intense period of activity of 1975 through 1978. She suffered in this calling of God as few women have. If any woman had justification to deny and turn against a former mate, Darlene would have that right.

Some two years after Darlene and I separated she completed her post graduate education with a Masters in Business. I and others were proud of her for her graduation! (That's me in the window shadow taking this picture!)

Chapter Thirty

Some Focus on **Year '77**

*Head note: In prior editing of this chapter I allowed a confounding
or confusion of experiences between the precognitive or remote
viewing and the then present scene in which I failed to note the
difference. I have revised this chapter to more fully distinguish
between those two different time frames. This chapter is loaded with
precognitive experiences. Page 165 of this book, the Boise Airport
incident illustrates this.*

In June of 1977, I made a trip to Utah again staying at the home
of John and Mary Fitzgerald. It was time to trigger a series of
events that I had seen happening to me. The middle of August
was set for trial on the church lawsuit seeking to permanently
enjoin me from Temple Square.

This was the International Year of Women. The Utah convention
was to be held at the Salt Palace in SLC. LaPriel James and
John Fitzgerald decided that a meeting needed to be held
concerning raising funds for my struggles since the one they had
started back in April broke up after Tricia Conner became "ill"
canceling the meeting. I never expected to really see any serious
money coming in and it never did. My expenses were my own to
pay!

It was agreed that we would hold a meeting at Denny's Diner in
South SLC alongside I-15. Interested persons were called and
invited. Relying on precognition*, I called Tricia She did not know
what to tell me as she had planned to take her sons camping for
the weekend. She told me she would think it over and call me
back.

Ten minutes later, Tricia called back with word she could make
the meeting. We met at the appointed hour. Very little if any real
discussion was had about fund raising. Tricia occupied the
moment with talk about the upcoming women's convention in
SLC. She made reference to Ezra Taft Benson's letter to the
President of the women's Relief Society instructing her how to

arrange for Mormon women to attend the convention and to defeat ratification of ERA (the Equal Right Amendment).

Tricia asked me if anything could be done to offset Benson's plans. I responded that there was. "Can I arrange a meeting with you and this other person who has influence in the Year of the Women organization in Utah," she asked. I told her I was heading west into California for a few days and that I would contact her by telephone. At the curb in front of Denny's she came on me with all the female charm she could muster. John was annoyed if not offended by the exchange between Tricia and me. "You be sure to call me," she said.

In West Sacramento, I stayed at the El Rancho Motel. I was there because of déjà vu I had experienced on the way to visit Roger Magleby, an undertaker in Vacaville. Magleby had contacted me in support of what I was doing. He also had a gripe about church attorneys squeezing tithing funds out of him that were owed by another individual. That person had assigned to the church, as tithing, a note owed him by Magleby.

While in Sacramento, the media reported the prison break of James Earl Ray from Bushy Mt. Prison in Tennessee. It had happened exactly as I had seen in the dreams earlier reported. This was confirmation to me that the sinister side of the Mormon Church through use of its agents in the FBI, was responsible for the killing of Martin Luther King, Jr. James Earl Ray was a patsy; a petty criminal set up to pay the price that should have been paid by others.

A day or so later, I was at Magleby's Funeral Home in Vacaville. I experienced more actualization of prior dreams Among these were helping Magleby place a Hispanic woman's clothed body in a casket; eating at a restaurant called the Coffee Tree; discovering Magleby's lie to me concerning his airplane**.

I had called Darlene on Thursday and asked her to meet me in Bend Friday evening at a certain motel. I told her I would be coming in late from Vacaville. I asked her to bring a gray wig and would she borrow the red Honda Civic from her DNS so that I could exchange mine with hers for a week.

189

The other precognitive testing concerned Tricia Conner. From a pay phone in the Coffee Tree, I also called Tricia on Thursday evening. I told her I would only be able to meet her in Boise at the airport on Saturday evening. She replied that she didn't know if she could be there. She attempted to discover my agenda but I was very vague. She then asked me to call the next evening, as she would see what plans she could make.

As arranged, I called the next day. This was Friday and again told her I could only meet her at the Boise airport at 7:30 PM on Saturday. She said she had been able to arrange a ride to Boise and was sure she could be at the airport on time. She wanted to know where to meet me. I told her in the lobby area of the terminal building, where we could find a place somewhere to discuss the ERA issue. "What if I get there before you do? Do you have a room," she asked. "No," I told her. If she planned to spend the night in Boise and arrived before me, she should book herself into a hotel to secure a room. "Where will we go? What will we do," she asked. "Oh, I want to spend some time with you. I think you are so wonderful. I want to absorb you, if you know what I mean," she added. I told her I knew exactly what she meant. She then told me she would be wearing a mini skirt, as she liked to be very feminine. In addition, she would be wearing a corsage on her blouse*** so that I would recognize her. My response was that she did not need to do that as I knew what she looked like.

Since I had already arranged to meet Darlene in Bend Friday evening for the car exchange, there was no way I could be at the Boise airport at 7:30 PM Saturday unless I left Bend early enough to make it on time.

Meeting with Darlene was an awkward experience. I had to tell her that I was maybe meeting Tricia at Boise Saturday evening. I know this not only shocked Darlene but also disappointed her for she had hoped for a weekend together.

I described Tricia to her and my suspicions that it would be an attempt to set me up. I told Darlene I would be very careful and follow déjà vu every step of the way****. It was important that Darlene know what was happening in case something went wrong and I would be arrested for solicitation. I was living it on the edge like in a James Bond movie. I have to admit though it was an exciting time!

It was with teary eyes that Darlene and I parted in Bend that Saturday morning. I asked her to look for the yellow pad notes when she arrived home. Since those notes in her own handwriting made reference to her two subsequent marriages, I figured she would have some comfort about the change that was taking place in our lives. She was unable to find them.

Assuming the trap being set for me in Boise failed; I would have a few days on my hands before the women's convention began in Salt Lake City. In fact, it was to be the following weekend.

I was going to be late in fact I was too late to make the time frame which I had stated to be there, so I stopped in route and called the airport. I asked them to page Tricia Conner on the intercom and asked them to convey the message that I was going to be late. Indeed I was late by over two hours.

Parking the red Honda in the airport parking lot, I went into the lobby area of the terminal building. Since I was late I did not wear the wig or sunglasses as I had initially intended as I felt that the trap would have failed time wise yet in the remote viewing there was a man with a wig and sunglasses whom I thought I was to copy. I was late and actually missed the events indicated by the prior remote viewing but I was there and had "Tricia" really been Tricia based on the courtesy telephone message which was never received, she would have remained for the meeting and I likely would have been entrapped. By the grace of God, I escaped that trap.

I had never been inside the Boise airport terminal building yet everything I saw was a recollection of the referenced dream of many months ago. I stopped to make a recall of that dream. It was much like re-experiencing the Lincoln Elementary epiphany of 1937.

As if by three dimensional holographic images I saw the police limousine arriving outside the front window. I saw a plain clothes man open the rear door and out stepped the Tricia trap. She was wearing a mini skirt and a corsage as Tricia said she would. However, she also wore dark glasses. From all appearances, it was Tricia. Entering the terminal building she was not alone. In fact, she was in the company of dark suited men that appeared to be Dainties or possibly, plains clothes police officers. Additionally there were several uniformed officers around the area.

When arriving passengers were coming down the escalator, "Tricia" would stand at the bottom as if to meet someone. During periods of waiting for a plane to arrive and its passengers come down the escalator, the group would be seated. These holographic images flashed on.

This went on for some time. As the PA system paged Tricia Conner to come to the courtesy telephone this "Tricia" did not move as if she had never been told her name for she never stirred. After a time, perhaps when the last incoming flight for the day had landed and the passengers debarked the group apparently gave up on my arriving down the escalator and disbanded. One or two remained a little longer. Upon disbanding, "Tricia" took off her glasses. Her face revealed the hard haggard face of a prostitute.

Everything including the white courtesy telephone on the wall was present as I had seen in that dream those many months earlier. I walked through the area even went up and down the escalators. Had "Tricia" been the real Tricia, she would have answered the page and would have remained to make the contact. But it was obvious this "Tricia" had been recruited by the Boise police to assist the SLCPD in setting me up for arrest, discredit or worse.

I booked into a Boise motel that night. The next day I went back to the airport to pick up déjà vu again. From there I drove a rather indirect route following precognition. If I did not see anything to confirm my position, I would stop and ponder things until something would indicate I continue. It seemed in many ways to be pointless yet I was on the trail following that which I had seen in the dream/precognition a year earlier. It was a testing of my ability to closely follow instruction.

The trail led me toward I-15. It was Sunday and I knew I was going to locate another motel where I would stay that night. The roof would be metal for I would hear rain on it. In addition, the walls would be thin, as I would hear a couple making love in the next unit.

Toward evening after much trial, and error, I found that motel. Everything happened as I had seen it including the metal roof and rain as well as the noises coming from the adjoining unit!

It was on 1-15 and not too far from Montana. It then happened that my precognitive dream about Louie's house in Great Falls would come to actualization. Louie was not there but his wife made me feel comfortable for a couple of days. I called Darlene from there to let her know that all was well and that I had survived the trap in Boise.

Afterwards I drove south to SLC stopping in Pocatello, Idaho overnight. The reader will remember Betty Moretti She was the nursing home entrepreneur who had asked to meet me way back on November 1st 1975. She also had her spiritual insight into my mission. At one time, she told me that there would be an attempt on my life She also mention that I would not complete my mission until after that event which she said would be thirty years away at least. She described the shooter and said that his shot would miss me. It would happen on the steps leading to the entrance of a large public building.

I also had such a dream. Because that event would trigger a public reaction, the sooner that it happened the better for I would be able to move forward on my mission. I longed to be free of it. I wanted to be able to lead a simple life and spend some time fishing. Despite the belief of some people, I was not on an ego trip. If the women's convention in SLC provided the scenario for the culmination, so be it. At Pocatello, I had some more déjà vu that would cause me to think that perhaps I was on that trail. I called my friend John Evans***** from Pocatello who according to the dream was supposed to be with me at that event. I was able to contact him but since he was tied up in commitments, it would be impossible for him to be in SLC with me. From there I drove to SLC. I went to Brian's office and conferred with him explaining the concerns about visiting the convention. He called his friends in the police department and they offered to provide me with security.

By this time, I was beginning to feel that this was not the occasion so I declined. I did make a brief solo visit to the Salt Palace where the convention was just underway. I recognized no elements of the scene or the building where the shooting was to happen. This was the first time on that two-week trek when I had no déjà vu about the current scene. With that settled, I drove home.

The experience/training of determinedly following precognition during this part of the mission saved my life and/or my reputation in an experience I would yet go through as recorded in Chapter Thirty Two *infra*.

A little over a week later, I contacted Portland Channel 2 reporter, Dean Jones. He made some inquiries among his associates in Boise and confirmed the large assembly of police at the airport that Saturday evening. He was told that there was an expectation that Ezra Taft Benson would be arriving and that the police were there to protect him. I did not see Benson of course but since my proposed meeting with Tricia was to overcome Benson's covert assault upon the upcoming women's convention, it figures he was used as bait for justification to discredit or possibly assassinate me had I played it as they thought I would.

Years later, in fact 16 years later, I received in the mail, a copy of the telephone conversation between Tricia in SLC and myself in Vacaville concerning the Boise event. It was on a cassette tape and heavily edited. In fact, the tape was made to appear that only one conversation occurred when in fact there were two.

Accompanying the tape was a typewritten transcript of the altered conversations as appearing on the tape. Included in the packet was an "analysis" of the conversation, which indicated that I had "obviously" fallen in love with Tricia but for some reason did not appear at the Boise airport. Since I had said (in previous writings) that I appeared and hadn't, it was obviously also a lie when I said (in other writings) that the Mormon Church was responsible for the assassination of Martin Luther King. The mailing had been forwarded to me by Jerald Tanner of SLC after he found it in his mailbox and correctly concluded it was the product of an illegal wiretap and he wanted nothing to do with it! The tape and wiretap confirms Tricia's complicity with the SLCPD.

[* In that precognition, I had seen Tricia call her superiors at SLCPD and tell them of my call and her dilemma about what to do. She did not want to disappoint her sons. She was told that the meeting to which she had been invited was far too important in their project to miss. Besides, she could take her sons camping next week.]

[** In following Déjà vu, I wanted to test the accuracy of precognition where I had asked him for use of his plane to fly to Boise. He responded by saying it was in the shop for repairs. Since that did not square with my dream, I went to the airport where I found it in a tie down area with other aircraft just as I had seen. I did not want the plane for I had other precognitive dreams of meeting Darlene in Bend, Oregon on this sojourn. I was simply testing accuracy of precognition for I knew my life would depend on it.]

[*** This was to cover the fact that someone who would have her build but not her face would impersonate her. In fact the person who appeared at the Boise airport wore dark glasses to hide her face Because of that, the plan was concocted of wearing a corsage to be certain to attract me. Why? For setting me up for arrest on charges of solicitation. This is an old Mormon trick and has been used many times before. In fact, a U.S. Congressman from Utah who had not gone along with Mormon politics had the same fate not too long before this attempt would be made on me.]

[**** Several months earlier, in another dream I saw myself driving through central Oregon. When awake, I told Darlene that I had just taken a road trip through the most exciting scenery of central Oregon. The circumstance of that dream had been exactly fulfilled by the visit to Vacaville and meeting Darlene in Bend. I had asked Darlene if her DNS had bought a new red Honda Civic. At that time, she had not. "Well she will." I exclaimed. "How do you know that," She asked. "Because I have seen myself driving it to Louie's in Great Falls,' I responded. Louie was Darlene's brother recently retired from the Air Force. Then there was a discussion about Louie living in Spokane. "Well he will be moving back to Great Falls," I replied. Indeed he did for he had bought stock in a

young growing commercial maintenance company that asked him to return to Great Falls and be an area supervisor. I was now following that trail of déjà vu. If I had taken the usual more direct route of highway 20, I would have been in Boise by 7:00 PM and likely, the trap set for me would have succeeded. By following the highway 26 route, I was delayed getting to Boise. Again precognition saved my life.]

[***** John Evans died on New Year's Day 2003???]

Chapter Thirty One

More Focus on Year '77

Early in the spring of 1977, I was contacted by a graduate student at the University of Utah. He was a freelance writer for *CRAWDADDY* magazine. He wanted to interview me for a feature article. His name was Bruce Margolious. When the magazine appeared on newsstands and in libraries in the summer of 1977, the cover depicted, in cartoon style, bees swarming around SLC. Bruce had capitalized on the one aspect I discussed with him concerning the microwave cavity resonator lapel pin worn to spy on unsuspecting persons. Since the article had a cartoon character about it, not much impact was felt by its appearance. However, Mormons did remove it from library shelves in some communities.

In referring to me, Bruce coined the statement "Prophet in Polyester" That was in reference to my wearing polyester slacks and jackets. At this time in the middle 70s, carefree synthetics were in vogue. For a traveling man it made life simpler. The contrast between my apparel and that of church elders and their attorneys made for quite a distinction. It was for me also a statement of disdain for pretension.

About a week after returning from the Vacaville-Boise episode, I received a letter from Tricia Conner explaining she was sorry I didn't make it to the airport and that perhaps the next time we met she would describe to me what the interior of the terminal building looked like! There was no anger for having stood her up. No explanation about the failure to discuss matters relating to the women's convention which was the ostensible reason for the meeting. No discussion about the "other" person who had an "in" with the Utah organization for the year of the women. Indeed, the tone of the letter suggested exactly that which I suspected and that which did in fact happen. I do not recall having responded to her, nor did I ever have contact with her again. However, Byron

Marchant, whom I will introduce later, had her hanging about him for a time as she did her undercover work for the SLCPD.

I believe, even at this late date, a sanitized federal investigative unit launched upon the mere basis of the self-indicting event of 1993 (the altered wiretap mailing) will gather enough evidence to indict individuals working for the "kingdom of God on earth"; i.e.; the Mormon Church hierarchy. I truly believe the purpose behind the Boise episode was to bring to light evidence sufficient to warrant that investigation. I believe we now have that evidence.

After the accidental shooting of Officer Olson, the big event of 1977 was the trial in Third District court on the complaint of the Corporation of the President of the Church of Jesus Christ of Latter Day Saints (Mormon) seeking to permanently enjoin me from Temple Square.

Brian had been successful through motion in court to disqualify Oscar McKonkie as counsel for the plaintiff. This was justifiable. McKonkie had attempted to bring Brian's bar membership under scrutiny and possible disbarment for the reason that a trust account check of Brian's had been returned for insufficient funds. The cause being the client check he had deposited into the account itself bounced and therefore the funds were not there to cover his check. This demonstrated the church's effort to disallow me counsel at trial.

As a result of that disqualification, the church hired an attorney who was not a part of the Kirten--McKonkie firm. His name was Alan Swan but he was a Mormon. The trial opened with Swan presenting the church case. That presentation relied heavily on my conduct in attempting to bring the issue of Black priesthood denial a year earlier at the April 1976 conference.

The church brought on a witness, a church employee, who testified he heard me say in the Tabernacle on that occasion, "Don't touch me I am the Lord". They argued that such conduct, as well as my attempt to hold a trial on the church leaders at the

next conference would be disruptive of religious services broadcast to the world.

198

When I was on the witness stand at behest of the church attorney, I took exception to the allegation that I said, "Don't touch me I am the Lord." What I had said was, "Get out of my way; you cannot stop the work of the Lord." I was asked if I thought the church president had to talk to me. My response was no but he should.

We got into a constitutional issue when Brian asked me if the church had a history when the president of the church was required to stand trial for misconduct before a priesthood tribunal (It of course did!). Swan objected because of the First Amendment, the court had no jurisdiction to hear that question. Civil courts were barred from hearing religious arguments based on the separation clause. After a break, the court ruled it did not have jurisdiction.

At the end of two days, the judge went into chambers for about ten minutes and emerged with a ruling that took him longer than that to read.

In effect, the court ruled that he had to balance the constitutional rights of both parties. I was permanently enjoined from going upon Temple Square at such times and under such circumstances as to interfere with the free exercise of religion of the plaintiff church. Notwithstanding that, the court ruled I could enter the premises at such times and under such circumstances when the free constitutional exercise of my religion would be present. In effect, there was no real injunction under a showing of constitutional right.

We appealed his ruling to the Utah Supreme Court. We were not unhappy with the ruling and the church thought it had prevailed. However, by appealing the ruling, it became a matter of recorded law when the decision of the Supreme Court was published.

After trial, it was necessary for Brian to go back to court to approve findings of fact which the court had ordered the plaintiff to prepare together with the form of the order. Again, the wording of my alleged statement, "Don't touch me I am the Lord," had been included as a finding of fact by Swan. Brian objected that exception had been taken and the church had presented only one witness. The court amended that finding to, "The defendant said something like, Don't Touch me...."

Such a finding is too vague to be a fact. This came after the Utah Supreme Court had included the prior quote in its dictum in the earlier partial appeal. As the reader will recall I have said previously in this book, that I filed an affidavit of prejudice against all members of the Utah Supreme Court because of that earlier prejudicial error.

At the hearing on the approval of finding of facts in the trial court, Alan Swan said, "If Wallace comes onto Temple Square the church would have him arrested." The court responded, "No they would not!" They would obtain an order from the court citing me into court to show cause why I should not be held in contempt for that conduct.

Oral arguments were heard before the Supreme Court in January 1979. Sometime later, it affirmed the lower court ruling which allows me under the correct circumstances, to hold trial on the church leaders. That right is now a matter of law in the State of Utah. It is still my intention to yet conduct that trial.

A few years later, Richard Bretzing*, the former Special Agent in Charge (SAC) of the FBI office in Los Angeles retired and became head of Mormon Church security. In the course of my keeping pressure on the church leaders that someday I will hold the promised trial on them, Mr. Bretzing cautioned me not to attempt to do so as he had been informed by church attorneys the church had a permanent injunction against my presence on Temple Square.

[I will detail later, a situation in which Mr. Bretzing went by the alias, Richard Garbutte, in dealing with me by telephone while he was still Special Agent in Charge(SAC) at Los Angeles.]*

I responded to Mr. Bretzing that the injunction was not a valid deterrent under the correct constitutional circumstances. He responded to that by issuing a letter of persona non grata (You are not welcome) on all church property. He then listed all property in the church block area including Temple Square. <u>He is wrong in the assumption that he can keep me off of Temple Square by a notice of persona non grata, when I know my constitutional right to be there exists</u>. His notice cannot overrule the special law on the matter upheld by the Utah Supreme Court.

If in fact I were to be there under those correct circumstances and they interfered with my rights by arrest or otherwise, they would be liable to me or my estate for the most horrendous damages.

During 1977, Preston Truman contacted me. He had waited until he felt that I might be the person to whom he should share information about Howard Hughes. It seemed that as a student in Enterprise, Utah in 1963, Preston had a dream one night. In the morning, he told his mother about it. The dream was seeing President John F Kennedy riding in a limousine and being shot and killed. After relating the dream, he went off to High School. That afternoon, his mother came to the school and asked that he be released for the day. In the car, she told Preston that President Kennedy had been shot just as he had described it in his dream.

It became the belief of Preston that the Mormon hierarchy was involved in that assassination. Over the years, Preston assembled a mass of information files to establish evidence that his contention of church involvement was correct.

Another aspect of Preston's research concerned Howard Hughes and the so-called Mormon Mafia led by Bill Gay. According to the information given me, Gay and his group had literally made a house captive of Hughes, enlarging and building on Hughes phobia of infection. In doing this, Gay was able to keep Hughes secreted from the world.

Going back in time, I recall a rumor flying around the corridors of the Mormon Church in the late 1950's that Hughes had willed his estate to the Mormon Church. That timing coincides with

Preston's contention that Hughes was effectively under control of the Mormon Mafia from the late fifties until his alleged body* was delivered to Houston, Texas for burial on April 5, 1976.

[It has been alleged by some that the body buried in an unmarked grave in Houston is not that of Hughes but a Vance Cooper who was a stand-in double for Hughes. Supposedly the body was identified by the FBI as that of Hughes but since there is heavy infiltration of the FBI by Mormons, it is most likely Cooper's body. Further, it fits more closely the story of Hughes having been killed at the time of the raid by "Intertel" on the Desert Inn Hotel in Las Vegas on Thanksgiving Day 1970. This all fits the "kingdom of god' agenda of the Church.}*

The reader will recall in chapter twenty-two, I said that during the trip to SLC on April 5,1976, I had a feeling that someone important had died and it later turned out to be Howard Hughes.

Preston introduced me to Mae Brussells, a Jewish woman living in Carmel, California. Mae was a conspiracy buff who had a weekly radio show at the local Carmel radio station. We talked a great deal about the Hughes connection with the Mormon Mafia.

An out growth of that introduction was the appearance of John H. Meier. John called me one Saturday afternoon in October of 1977. He praised me for having the courage and fortitude to take on the Mormon Church. John had been an aide to Howard Hughes but was excluded from the inner circle of the Mormon Mafia after the Intertel take over of the Desert Inn in Las Vegas on Thanksgiving Day 1970.

The next year, Summa Corporation, which Bill Gay had created allegedly without the knowledge or approval of Hughes, sued John in Utah Federal District Court in an attempt to quiet John. I will deal with John in a subsequent chapter.

Another strange connection was made with Don Goodwill of Portland, Oregon. Don had contacted me because he believed the Mormon Church was behind estate usurpation in Eastern Oregon. An estate had been taken over and the lawful heirs denied their inheritance. The large estate was used to grow potatoes. The proceeds of that production were alleged by Don to have ended up in the Mormon Church.

I was also introduced to a Reverend Charles Bean of Eugene, Oregon who told a story about his charitable organization having located a large uranium deposit* in Southern Utah. That story was one of intrigue involving not only the Mormon Church but also allegedly, the Utah Corporation. The Utah Corporation has license to mine the face of Australia. According to Bean, Lyndon B. Johnson was implicated as a trustee of a teamsters trust fund in Lubbock Texas. Johnson was alleged to have used the trust fund to pay for the mining of the ore which was packaged in barrels and shipped to Australia under the care of the Utah Corporation.

[* In the late fifties, about the same time the rumor of Howard Hughes having willed his estate to the Mormon Church, another rumor flew around the grapevine of the church. That rumor was the church had discovered a very large deposit of uranium in Southern Utah. At the time my question was, "What the hell does the church want with uranium? An easy answer has to do with the quest for empire as the "kingdom of God on earth".]

According to the story, the shipping was done on old liberty ships taken from the Vallejo harbor mothball fleet in San Fransico Bay. Bean was in position at that time to requisition those ships.

Bean also indicted that in addition to the ships used by the Utah Corporation, two liberty ships were used in the Bay of Pigs invasion of Cuba. These ships were renamed the "Houston" and the "Barbara" and were under license to Zapata Offshore Oil Corporation owned by George Bush, former CIA Director and later Vice President and President of the United States.

According to the story, one of the liberty ships was in London harbor laden with uranium ore when it was hijacked by Israeli agents and taken to Israel. That Uranium provided Israel with the raw materials to develop their atom bomb.

At the time of the alleged conspiracy, Federal law forbade exportation of uranium from the U.S.. Immediately upon assuming the Presidency in November 1963; Johnson pushed legislation to allow for exportation of uranium. He introduced the programs "Atoms for Peace" and "Atoms for Food" (the by-product of refinement was a fertilizer). That legislation allowed for the shipments of uranium to Australia* and the arranged hijacking in London.

[In the early 1980's, when uranium ore was several times expensive as it was in as the late 50's. It was reportedly shipped back to the U.S. at an extremely high profit.]*

Before Johnson announced in 1968 that he would not run for President again, he made a 3-day whirlwind tour of the world and discovered the violations of the uranium exportation laws, which he had promoted. It was that discovery which led him to abandon another term in office. Many have believed his heart attack a few years later was chemically induced to silence him

The Utah Corporation later had several of its liberty ships confiscated when President Allende nationalized the mining industry in Chile.

Betty Moretti died in January or February 1977 because of mysterious internal bleeding. She had been taken to the University of Oregon Medical Hospital in Portland. The illness came on her at age 64 after her partners, medical doctors from the Beaches area of California (and Mormons) had visited with her. Whether she had told them of her association with me can only be speculated.**

*** UPDATE: On July 14th of 2009 while on a trip to Oregon, I was motivated to travel to Lebanon, Oregon to search out the history of Betty Moretti. I was unable to find trace of her name or work or former nursing home in Lebanon, Oregon. So far attempts to locate her death certificate have failed. I am beginning to get the feeling of foul play in her death if indeed she did die as it was reported to me.*

Chapter Thirty Two

Subterfuge in Shelton

Don Benson was a Real Estate Broker in Shelton, Washington. Shelton is an old logging community on the extreme western part of lower Puget Sound. It lies to the west of Olympia the Capital of Washington State. I became associated with Don because of Sharon and Marion Wright having moved to the area in late 1976. Sharon was a licensed sales agent for Don.

At the time of the April 1977 conference of the Mormon Church, I had been remodeling an old plumbing shop building into office suites for Don. It was while working there that I received the call from Dave Briscoe about the church having obtained the second non-noticed TRO designed to keep me off Temple Square.

After I came back from SLC and between the events of the first half of 1977, I finished off the remodeling. Later, in the fall of that year, Don wanted me to design and build a home for him on Harstine Island. It would be across the waterway from Marion and Sharon's. Additionally I had been introduced to a couple, Ralph and Peggy Baldwin. He was a retired naval officer. They purchased a lot from Don; two lots east of the lot on which he wanted me to build him a home. Both of these lots were on the waterfront.

I designed both of the houses and later I would build Don's house while Marion would build the other. The planning took place between November of 1977 and the spring of 1978. The lot between those two projects had been promised to be sold to me for construction of a house for Darlene and me. Later however, Don sold it to someone else never explaining why he broke his promise.

Early in January, I met with Don in his office in Shelton to review the plans for his home. Don was suffering from heart conditions and wanted to set things up for his wife so she would be financially comfortable in the event he should die.

At that meeting Don said to me, "A strange thing has happened, I have been offered a really good price for this building." "By whom," I asked. "Well it is a broker over on the coast," he replied. I told him that was great to go ahead and sell it. "I don't know that I can" he replied to which I asked," why not?"

"There are some things that I will have to do and I don't know that I can," He said. Puzzled, I attempted to find out what those things were. It was no secret that Don knew I was surviving on deja vu. I had told him about the dream precognitions, which I experienced. At this point he said," Have you ever had any of those dreams about me?" Giving it some thought I answered, "No."

He then said I would be surprised whom it was that wanted to buy his building. After teasing him about it, he let me know the buyer was the Mormon Stake President in Aberdeen. Throughout that year and into early 1979, many strange things happened in Shelton. .

I had become acquainted with Michael Culliton; a friend of Sharon Wright, Mike was a veteran of Vietnam. He had been shot up several times during the war and returned three times to work as a sapper behind enemy lines. Mike later acted as my bodyguard at times. He was very well built and was Black Belt Karate

Mike wanted to pursue a dream he had about a lobster fishery in the Marshall Islands. In January 1978, he went to Honolulu to meet with a fisheries agent from the Marshall Islands government. Don Benson was interested in investing with Mike and funded the trip for Mike. While he was there, Don wanted me, as an attorney, to meet with that agent, a Hawaiian, to assess the situation.

Don* funded my travel to Honolulu where I met the fisheries expert from the government of the Marshal Islands. It was my first trip to Hawaii and I enjoyed it very much. The assessment was that the project looked viable but more research would have to be given to it.

[Looking back on it, Don had a project to complete regarding me and his amiability was a part of that objective which later he shared with me.]*

Don kept pressing me to establish a law practice in Shelton. I repeatedly told him there were already more than enough attorneys in town. At one point during the January meeting when the subject came up and I answered as usual when he asked me, "What if something should happen to one of the attorneys so that a vacancy would open?" I laughed and asked if one of them was going to be bumped off. There was no sensible reason why he should have such an interest.

Later, Don had me draw plans for a two-unit commercial office building to be built on a lot in town, which he owned. He wanted to get a commitment from me to occupy the second unit as a law office. Again, I refused to commit.

In early March, I received a call from John Meier in Delta B.C. Canada. John wanted me to come to Vancouver where he would transfer to my custody some copies of the Howard Hughes papers which Mexican police had confiscated in the Acapulco penthouse when word of Hughes death in Houston was announced.

I traveled by car to Vancouver where I received those papers. I came back across the border at Blaine then I flew to Carmel California for a weekend going over the papers with Preston Truman and Mae Brussells. I kept a few copies of the documents turning the rest over to Preston for preservation in his vault in Utah. I will deal more with this later.

After I began a monthly newsletter for the LDS Freedom Foundation some time late in 1977, I would take one day a month to work on it. There were no computers or word processing back then; at least not PCs, as we know today. I had a correctable ribbon typewriter. I never learned to type so just used two fingers (the same as I am in writing this book). It was an ordeal for me. I had no editor and no time to spend on review.

It was a one-day a month effort and what came out on the first draft was it.

In January or February of 1978, I converted from a newsletter to a magazine format. It was called the Millennial Messenger. Converting to a magazine format made it even more arduous. I still only had the one-day period. Therefore, in March I converted to a two-month publication. Oddly, the last publication was the March-April edition. It was called the Conference Edition to be published and circulated in time for the April conference of the church.

That edition has been cited by some as causing a great deal of consternation for the church leaders. It contained an Intrigue Report where all of the sinister information I had been receiving was published. It cast the church in a very bad light from the standpoint of being a Christian Organization. The other articles including one by Byron Marchant* challenged the intelligence of the church in its posture toward the Black priesthood issue.

[Byron had made his own waves with the church when he caused a lawsuit to be filed against the church by the American Civil Liberties Union (ACLU) for discriminating against black scouts in church controlled scout troops.]*

After subscriptions were mailed, I took a hundred or so copies of the Messenger to April conference in SLC. These were distributed free of charge to anyone who would accept them. Byron Marchant was arrested on Temple Square for handing them out to conference goers. He was handcuffed and pushed into the back of a police car and taken to jail. The charge was trespass on Temple Square yet he had never been served with notice of persona non grata. A lot of publicity was given to this unchristian action by church security. Eventually, the church being embarrassed dismissed the charges.

I made no attempt to enter Temple Square or to give prior notice to hold the trial of the Brethren at the square. I remember walking down Main Street away from the square with several supporters including John F. and also having my "old friend", Detective Stoner of SLCPD in the group. Stoner made a comment about the possibility of some red neck shooting me while I demonstrated outside the Square. I told him, "If that is what God wants done, so be it!" Apart from the March-April

Messenger being made available at Temple Square I kept low key at this time.

In April, I began the construction of Don's house. This would prove to be a long drawn out effort. Apart from my being gone a lot, obtaining performance of subcontractors was difficult. Don was his own contractor hiring me to build it for him. The same arrangement happened with Marion and Ralph Baldwin.

The twin cities of Chehallis and Centrialia lie about 30 miles south of Olympia. They lie to the north of Vancouver by about 70 miles and are parallel to and connected by Interstate 5. Shelton is farther north and west.

At the time, Darlene was acting administrator for a nursing home in Centralia. This was a part of her trouble shooting activity for a nursing home operator after the ordeal in Portland's Hillhaven nursing home. On the 9th of June, I was on my way to Shelton so I stopped by to visit her there

When I went into her office, she was on the telephone but she put her hand over the receiver and said, "Have you heard the news?" Since I had not, I said, "what news?" "The Mormons have given priesthood to black men!"

I was elated! The news had just come over the radio. After some congratulations, I left and drove to Shelton. Arriving at Don Benson's office there were two telephone calls waiting for me. The media from around the country, mostly radio stations, wanted to interview me. I was on the telephone continually for several hours.

One of the last calls was from a reporter for KIRO TV 7 in Seattle. I knew the church owned the station. The reporter wanted to interview me. I arranged to meet with him at the Tyee Motor Lodge in Tumwater.

Leaving Shelton, I drove back toward Vancouver. Tumwater is just south of Olympia. I told the reporter I would meet him in the coffee shop. I was there when he arrived. He wanted to do the interview outside if I did not mind. Outside on the grass there were two vans. The television crew had unloaded a lot of equipment in black boxes and a satellite dish was present.

I had been interviewed on television a number of times. In each case, there was the reporter and a cameraman. The reporter held a mike and a recorder. Never before was there so much equipment present. I knew the brethren in SLC were viewing me live.

"Now that the church has given priesthood to Black men, does that mean you will discontinue your efforts against the church." he asked. I answered by saying a resounding, "NO."

Being taken back, he asked me, "why not?" I told him I had become the hub of an information wheel having learned a lot of sinister activity in which the church was engaged. I told him I would not quit until I saw the church leaders indicted and sent to prison for their criminal conduct against Howard Hughes.

My statement dumbfounded the reporter. He said he knew nothing about that and admitted he had been a member of the church for just a short while. As you can imagine, the interview was very brief. I drove back to Vancouver where I spent a good deal of the weekend being interviewed by local media.

While working on Don's house, I rented a small apartment at Jerrell's Cove, an inlet on the Sound about a half mile away. I would stay there at night and some weekends not going back to Vancouver.

During the night of June 14th, at Jerrell's Cove, I had a vivid dream* It started by seeing a man park a car in front of a

two-story office building in downtown Shelton. He got out carrying a shoe box. He went around the side disappearing into a doorway that had a sign over it with an arrow pointing up like a staircase. The sign said "Attorney"

[* The intensity of this experience was so great that today [2000], 22 years later, it is still vivid.]

The next scene was from behind a man seated at a desk in what appeared to be a law office. Across the desk was seated the man who had just parked his car. This man made the statement, "I am told that you can be a confidential source of information." The attorney responded by saying, "That depends on the fee."

At that moment, the visitor took the lid off the shoe box spreading a large quantity of currency across the desk.

"Does that look like enough," was the question, to which the attorney replied, "That looks adequate." The conversation then went like this:

Visitor: "Is **there an attorney in town that is more**

disliked than others?"

Atty: **"Yes"**

Visitor: "**If something should happen to this**

attorney, would there be much of a stir to

investigate?"

Atty: **"Probably Not. He and the Prosecuting**

Attorney are arch enemies. They hate each

other's guts. They have been contending

against each other for years over the office.

one will be elected for a term and then the other

will beat him out at next election. The

prosecuting attorney is also the County

Coroner. I doubt very much if there would

be any inquiry if he should turn up dead."

Visitor: "**That's a lucky piece of information. Is this attorney married?**"

Atty: "**Yes, he has a wife.**"

Visitor: "**Do they get along?**"

Atty: "**Hell no! They fight like cats. Even at socials they will fight in front of everyone. It's well known they don't get along.**"

Visitor: "**Sounds like I have hit pay dirt here!**"

The next scene I saw was that of a meeting between the visitor and an attractive dark haired woman perhaps in her forties. She gives a handgun to the visitor. Their dialogue went like this:

Visitor: "**Do you have anywhere you could go? Any thing you could do for a while?**"

Woman: "**Well, my sister runs a hostel to Europe every summer. She has wanted me to go with her but I have never done it.**"

Visitor: "**You go this time! You need to be out of the way when this happens.**"

The next scene is inside a garage. A man in a business suit enters the garage. Immediately behind him, the visitor emerges

212

from the shadows. He has a gun in his hand, which he puts to the back of the man's head.

Visitor: " **Don't turn! Do as I say! Put the**

palms of your hands under your chin"

"Now I want you to place your elbows on

The hood of the car and press down hard

With your chin. Harder! Harder!

HARDER!"

As this was happening, the victim's head went backwards as the weight of his body was transferred to his chin so much so that the hood of the car became dimpled. The gun behind the man's head was also pressing into the base of his skull.

Visitor: **"HARDER!**

That will do nicely."

BAM!

The gun fired sending a bullet into the brain, the body of the man slumped to the floor.

That was all I saw. I pondered this for a few days. Next Saturday June 17th, Darlene came up with Darren to Jerells Cove for the weekend. I related to her the dream. She was terribly frightened. I assured her the attorney was not me.

Prior to June 8th, when the Mormon Church gave priesthood to Black men, Marion and Sharon Wright had been having serious marital problems. Marion had quietly been removing his tools and personal things from the home he had remodeled and shared with Sharon. I was privy to this but was asked not to say anything to Sharon.

Two weeks before June 9th, Sharon called me. She said Marion had left her and did I know where he went. It turned out that Marion and Mike Culliton had traveled to Hawaii. While they were there, they saw headlines in the Honolulu paper of the church collapse on the Black priesthood issue.

Sharon suspected Marion had gone to Hawaii and a few days later went there herself. Their paths crossed and Marion returned home. He was determined to get a divorce. He asked me if I would help him find an attorney. I called attorney Jim Sawyer, making an appointment. Marion wanted me to accompany him.

The appointment was set for 1:00 PM on Wednesday June 21st. Sawyer was late. In fact very late by almost an hour. When he appeared behind his desk, he apologized. There had been a terrible event that morning. Local attorney John Ragan had committed suicide in his garage with a gunshot to the back of his head.

As he related the details, my mind went to the dream of a week earlier. I told Sawyer about it and even the name of the attorney who had given the information to what could only be described as a professional hit man. Sawyer intimated that that attorney would do most anything for money. Not long after the death of Ragan, a Super 8 Motel would be built in Shelton. The attorney who I had seen giving the information owned it.

Later, Jim Sawyer said to me, "Ragan really learned his business when he was Prosecuting attorney and Coroner. He angled the handgun very precisely behind his head to be sure of instant death!" How did the investigation learn that? There was an impression in the hood of the car where he had put his elbow!

Ragan was taken to the local hospital were he was pronounced dead. About 5 years later, I had the opportunity to meet the head nurse of the emergency room of that hospital. She told me she was on duty the morning John Ragan was brought in. I asked her if she believed it was a suicide. She responded with a resounding, NO!**

Everything about the shooting I learned was identical to what I had seen. It was not suicide but murder. What happened later proved that to me beyond any doubt.

John Ragan's wife was in Europe with her sister at the time. Although word was sent to her about the tragedy, I understand it took her five days to return home.

Shortly after the death of Ragan, Don Benson began to intimate that now there was a vacancy in the legal profession In Shelton, why did I not think about acquiring his law office. I did not want to get back into law practice. I was on a mission and while I had to earn some money to fund it, I did not want to be tied down with a law practice.

I met John Ragan's widow sometime later at the urging of Benson to check out the office. She was seated behind her deceased husband's desk in the rented office. There was not much there.

An old freestanding steel safe, old office furniture and law books that were out of date except Washington Reports, which had been updated.

At that time, Ragan's widow was asking a very high price for the office. Many recent bar admittees had passed the summer bar and were interested in the office. By law, neither an attorney nor his heirs can sell client files. So literally there was nothing of value to a purchaser. The furniture could have been bought at yard sales for less than two hundred dollars and the books had little if any value. Yet, she wanted many thousands of dollars for the lot. It was obvious to me she did not intend to sell to just anyone.

Don had told me the day after the death of Ragan, that in spite of his having a lousy reputation in Shelton he could not have been that bad because he had been appointed a Federal Magistrate. I asked his widow if he had ever been an U.S. Magistrate and she said no. I was never able to confirm it either way. Since I believed this was a part of some conspiracy to set me up, there was no interest on my part to get involved at least at that time.

As time went on Don kept insisting that I get into the practice of law. I learned that some of the prominent members of the community were beginning to badmouth me behind my back.

Another dream had happened to me and I saw a group of men discussing strategy to get me established in the law office. "Get old (Blankity) to contact Wallace. He is always suing somebody and he could likely induce Wallace to represent him."

One fellow, a perennial law suit challenger of acts by Mason Country even came out to Benson's house while I was working on it to attempt to get me to act as his attorney. I listened to him and then told him no. I recited the Serenity Prayer to him and suggested there were things that he could not change and to accept it.

Because of the dream, I was aware and on top off all that effort, the fellow that came out to the job site was the one they

had sent. A few weeks later he talked to my son in Vancouver by telephone and wanted to know if I had changed my mind about being his attorney.

Within five minutes of the man leaving, Don Benson showed up with an eager expression on his face. Was I going to help this man? I told him I was not. It was obvious to me that Don was a participant in the conspiracy.

Once or twice I would run into Don at a fast food restaurant in Shelton. He would ask me to guess who he had just met with. I did not know and so he would tell me the Mormon broker from Aberdeen who wanted to buy his office. I told him to sell it and he would again remind me there were things he had to do first. I knew the things he had to do were getting me to settle into the practice of law. I also knew I never would.

After Marion had finished Baldwin's, house I had him help me to finish Don's. On October 31st I went to Vancouver B.C. to meet John Meier. I will deal with Meier in the next chapter.

When I returned, Marion excitedly wanted to talk to me. It appeared that morning when Marion was at the equipment rental yard getting some tools for work on Don's house, the former manager of the Mason County Credit Union stopped him in the street. Marion was asked, "Are you still friends with Doug Wallace?" Marion told him he was and then Marion was asked to participate in the distribution of drugs. This totally shocked Marion.

"These drugs are clean they have already been confiscated," Marion was told. Marion made no commitment but said he would think it over. He was given the names of several prominent individuals living in Shelton who were involved. Once, when we were both working on Benson's house one of those individuals came out from Shelton to talk to Marion. He wanted to talk to Marion in private so they went outside the sliding door to the deck where they walked and talked. After that person left, Marion told me it was just more effort to recruit him to become involved with drug trafficking. I suggested to Marion that he play it cool.

It appeared to me a part of the conspiracy was to set me up for discredit and possible criminal action for drugs. I called John Meier in Canada about the problem and he said he would contact his people in the FBI. The next day while at Benson's office I received a call from the F.B.I. SAC in Seattle. He began to rattle on about referencing John Meier. I told him I did not know who he was and would not talk to him over the telephone. He paused and said, "Of course." I was told to wait, he would think it out, and someone would get back to me.

Later, I received a call from an FBI agent who said his name was Richard Garbutte. He told me to call directory assistance and get the telephone number of the FBI in Los Angeles then to call that number and ask for Richard Garbutte. (I am not sure of the spelling) I did that and we had several conversations over the next few weeks. Nothing ever came of it and I became certain that Garbutte was implicated with Mormon interests. It is my contention today that Garbutte was in fact Richard Brezting, Los Angeles SAC who became Mormon Security chief after his retirement. I have told him so and he has never denied it.

Marion and I would have lunch occasionally at a tavern on the highway that circled Harstine Island. It was probably three miles from the job site. One day we were having lunch at the large round table just inside the front door. We were talking about the conspiracy, when a stranger came into the bar. He seated himself at the bar not more than five feet from where we sat.

Marion made a comment, "I hope we don't have a Judas in here." He was referring to his son in-law seated to his right. I replied, "Yes we do; and he sits right there." I was pointing to the stranger at the bar. That man was the very person I had seen in the dream of the murder of John Ragan. He heard me and arose from his seat going over to the pool room side of the tavern. He picked up the cue ball and threw it at the racked billiard balls. They exploded all over the room. He then left knowing I had fingered him. I never saw him again but he wore a brown suede jacket and looked like one of the individuals photographed at the Kennedy assassination whom the Congressional Special Committee on Assassinations was looking for.

About this same time, I had become very suspicious of the way Garbutte was handling the matter of the drug dealing. At one point, he sent me to a DEA (Drug Enforcement Agency) officer with my story but again there was no movement. Garbutte had told me he was doing everything to help John Meier but even that proved to be misleading (more about that later)

I decided to make a personal contact with the special agent in charge (SAC) of the Seattle FBI office. I called him from Vancouver and arranged to meet him at a hotel near his office. I had long lost trust in the FBI because of the Mormon presence in it. For that reason, I suggested the hotel meeting. Arriving at the hotel, I placed a call and left a message as to where I would be.

He did not appear but several suspicious looking men became visible around the hotel lobby.

I descended into the basement of the hotel where there were shops. I went into a shoe shine cubicle and seated myself on a chair. No sooner had I done that than two of these dark suited men appeared in the doorway. They mounted chairs on each side of me. The attendant began to work on the shoes of the man to my left. As he did so, the younger man on the right began to sweat as he put his finger into the neck of his shirt. He was looking down at his shoes and they were suede!

I left both of them there and went up the staircase to the second floor, I traveled across the skyway connecting the hotel to the parking garage and took the elevator of the parking garage up to the top floor and then I walked down the inside staircase to the third floor where my pickup was parked. Inside the pickup there was another suit hanging. Quickly I changed my suit.

While doing that, the metal fire door opened as it echoed in the garage. I peeked out the window to see another of the dark-suited men standing in the open doorway looking around for me. Not seeing anyone, he went back inside the stairwell.

Later I went back over to the hotel and left another message at the FBI office saying I did not like what had happened and I would be leaving. This was one of the few times when I was overcome by paranoia.

Mike Culliton came to my rescue having me stay the night at his house. Had anyone attempted to break in there that night one or more of them would have died on the spot. Some few days later, I was told I should have just gone up to the FBI office and not have attempted to meet the SAC at the hotel. I did not then trust the FBI and I still do not to this day. That is a sad commentary on what is supposed to be the elite law enforcement branch of government.

Towards the completion of Don's house, one Saturday afternoon, I was spraying lacquer on the doors and woodwork. I heard Don come in the front door and he began to choke and cough due to the fumes. I shut off the spray equipment and talked with him. A few days earlier, I had been speaking to Don's wife, Velma. I told her about my suspicions regarding an attempt to set me up. I suggested to her that Don was at least on the perimeter of it if not fully involved.

Don was upset that I had talked to Velma about the conspiracy. He did however admit there was a conspiracy to get me into Ragan's office. He also admitted that at least Five Hundred Thousand Dollars had been spent on the conspiracy. And so what, If he and I played our coins right we could both make some money from it! Again, I told him I would not be practicing law in Shelton.

The next morning being Sunday, I was in the Capitol Restaurant (actually next door to the empty Ragan office) having breakfast. Don came in and sat across the table from me. He swore a little and told me he wanted to make some money to leave for Velma when he died. That I needed to make some money for an inheritance for my young son. I asked him how was that going to be done. He told me I had to open a law office in Shelton. I said, "You mean you want to build the two suite office building?" "NO," was his reply. "I mean next door in the Ragan law office."

My first question of him was how would that make him any money. He then said we had talked about it the day before. He suggested since I knew what was coming down I could go ahead and buy the office so he could make some money. I could be careful and avoid the trap.

I then told him Ragan's widow wanted too much money. He indicated that was not a problem. How much would I be willing to pay for it? "Nothing, I don't want it. Besides I have no money," was my answer. He then asked if I would be willing sign a note for Four Thousand Dollars to purchase it. "Well, I would have no intention of ever paying it off because its all junk," I said. He said he would negotiate with Ragan's widow that day and meet me there, in the Capitol Restaurant, that evening. After a day of work on his house I was again at the restaurant

Don and Velma were already there. He had a grin on his face from ear to ear. He had arranged with Ragan's widow for me to buy the office [equipment] for the note. Could I meet her at her attorneys the next evening after work? So there it was. Ragan's widow had held out on all kinds of cash offers from new bar admittees; had held the price at over Ten Thousand Dollars and was now willing to sell it to me for a note for Four Thousand Dollars!

At Ragan's widow's attorney's office I signed the note and was given the keys to the office. She was very nervous, even shaking as the papers were signed. What was promised her I do not know. Neither do I know what Don was promised. However, as it turned out neither of them profited from the death of John Ragan because I did not open the office or practice law in Shelton. Nor did I honor the note***.

Don's house was finished before Christmas. I left Shelton, not returning for some time. The entire episode in Shelton, beginning with the effort to lure me into the practice of law in January 1978, and ending in December, was the product of sinister Mormon thought. It matters not, that the conspiracy to murder John Ragan involved Church security, FBI and CIA, the ultimate responsibility lies at the doors of church leadership. It is their maddened dream which precipitated the event.

** Several years later in 1986, I had occasion to be in Shelton Washington At that time I attempted to obtain the Coroner's files on the Ragan "suicide". This was eight years after the fact and the file was still sealed by the DA/Coroner.

*** Ragan's Widow gave the note to a legal firm in Olympia for collection. Later she called me about paying the note and I responded that she would have to sue me as I would not pay it based on the dream that she was implicated in the death of her husband. She laughed at that assertion saying it was a "silly thing". I was looking for a legal way to make discovery. However no attempt at collection was ever made.

Gunshot takes life of attorney John C. Ragan

John C. Ragan, 47, a Shelton attorney, was found dead at his home in the Walker Park area Wednesday morning of an apparently self-inflicted gun shot wound, Coroner Byron McClanahan said.

McClanahan said he and the Mason County Sheriff's Office were continuing the investigation of the death to determine if the fatal wound was accidentally or intentionally inflicted.

Death was caused, the coroner said, by a single gun shot wound. The wound was just

behind the ear, McClanahan said.

The weapon and the gun was one which Ragan kept in his home.

The body was discovered behind the family home in the victim's car, Corp. about 9 a.m. Wednesday. Ragan was brought to Mason General Hospital by ambulance where he died about 10 a.m.

McClanahan said he had made some arrangements for an autopsy which was to be performed Wednesday night.

The coroner said there was no sign of a struggle where the

body was found. Ragan's glasses had fallen off and were bent, he said.

McClanahan said that no note was found either in the home or Ragan's office.

Investigation so far, McClanahan said, had turned up no reason for Ragan to have taken his own life. The investigation will continue, he said.

Ragan came to Shelton in 1961 to open his law practice after graduating from the University of Washington Law School. He first shared an office

with Attorney Glenn Correa, and later opened his own office in the Title Insurance Building.

He was appointed city attorney shortly after coming to Shelton and served in that capacity for about five years.

He was elected Prosecuting Attorney in 1966 and served a four-year term in that office.

He was a candidate for District Court Judge and served on numerous occasions as District Court Judge Pro-tem.

He is survived by his wife, Carolyn, one daughter and two sons.

John C. Ragan

Burglary charge is filed

Charges of second degree burglary in Mason County Superior Court were filed this week against Mark David Adams, 19, Rt 4 Box 829, Shelton.

The Shelton-Mason County Journal

Thursday, June 22, 1978   Ninety-second Year - Number 25   5 Sections - 44 Pages   15 Cents Per Copy

Monday, July 31, 1978   ©The Columbian 1978, Vancouver, Washington (206) 694-3391

Investigators want information on these men. See story below. (AP)

Mystery men names sought

WASHINGTON (UPI) — Millions of Americans were asked for help today in identifying blurred photographs and sketches of mystery men connected to the murders of John F. Kennedy and Dr. Martin Luther King Jr.

The Assassinations Committee Sunday made public two composite drawings and three blurred photographs "to make best possible use of available pictorial evidence and holographic techniques ... in the ope that citizen recognition of them might shed additional light on the assassinations of ... Kennedy and

[LDS] recognizing any of the men

depicted were asked to contact the House Select Committee on Assassinations, Washington, D.C. 20515, and submit any pictures they may have of the subjects.

Proven linkage of any of the men to the Kennedy and King cases case would directly challenge the still unrelated conclusion by the Warren Commission that Lee Harvey Oswald acted alone in killing Kennedy in Dallas Nov. 22, 1963; and the guilty plea by escaped convict James Earl Ray that he murdered King in Memphis, Tenn., April 4, 1968.

Ray is serving a 99-year sentence at Brushy Mountain Prison at Petros, Tenn., but has since changed his story

and is trying for a new trial on grounds he was the "fall guy" for a mysterious Canadian smuggler named "Raoul" who never has been identified.

A series of public hearings is scheduled on both cases in August, September, November and December, when all "new" evidence will be reviewed and many witnesses, including Ray, will be recalled for testimony.

The three photographs released by the committee Sunday included a blurred image of a dark-haired man, possibly with mustache, sitting on a curb with a group whose faces do not show. The committee caption said only that the picture was taken in Dealey Plaza "moments after President Kennedy was shot."

The other two photographs, according to the committee, are "of two men who may have been in Mexico City in the fall of 1963 when Lee Harvey Oswald ... was there."

One photograph shows a handsome, apparently blond-haired man in his 20s or early 30s. The other photograph, badly scratched and blurred, is a side shot of a light or gray-haired, aquiline-nosed man who could be in his late 40s or 50s.

An older version of the man on the right (arrow) would resemble the man seen in a dream 47 days before this article appeared. I saw the man asking questions of a Shelton attorney and again being given a gun by a woman. I also saw the man in reality when he appeared at the lunch tavern on Harstine Island in November and left when I blew his cover described on page 218 infra.

He was wanted in connection with the JFK assassination.

Chapter Thirty Three

Hughes, Meier and Mormons

What happened? All I did was ordain a Black man! This was a purely religious matter. Before I knew it, I was having strange experiences. It began to appear as though the ban on Black priesthood was but a scab covering a cesspool of Mormon corruption. Is that what God had intended since the 8th birthday experience? Certainly, the direction to ordain Larry had no overt plan to expose the sinister side of Mormonism. But that is exactly what happened

The decision to assassinate an attorney, any attorney in Shelton although being in the planning since January of 1978 was delayed until after the church first gave in on the Black priesthood ban. They wanted to see if I was satisfied enough by that action for me to quit my probing into their sinister activities.

The question asked of me in Tumwater on the 9th of June, "Would I now cease my activities against the church," came too late. When I said, "No," they put into final play the plot, which resulted in the death of John Ragan

Oddly, Black priesthood was a negotiable item, but exposing their agenda for one world government was not. They never understood then and do not to this day that my mission was not my own but that of God. I am merely a tool, an instrument. Not understanding the true nature of God, they do not understand matters of the spirit for they are far too pragmatic and wordily. They know that the Kingdom of God on earth is a physical, worldly kingdom and therefore it must be brought about by pragmatic methods such as cunning, deception and murder.

As a result of my seemingly accidental intrusion into the arena of their political escapades, they began to deal with me in a pragmatic way. It did not dawn on them then and it does not today that their concept of "kingdom" is archaic. They of course are not alone in this mistaken notion.

For purposes of protecting the integrity of church authority, security operatives are common in all cult organizations. We saw them in the Bhagwan Rajneesh phenomenon that took over Antelope Valley in Oregon in the 80's; we saw them in Jonestown in the 70's. We see them today in Montana at Elizabeth Prophet's establishment.

Armed security in Mormonism was very visible in the beginning from Missouri to Illinois and then on to Utah. Orrin Porter Rockwell, never a member of the Mormon Church, was nonetheless the hired gun of Joseph Smith, Jr. and Brigham Young. He was paid in his failed attempt to kill Missouri Governor Lilburn Boggs*. He was used by Young to collect the wages due the Mormon Battalion as the pioneers trekked across the plains

[Governor Boggs has been accused of issuing an extermination order against the Mormons. Research shows that it was Sidney Rigdon who began the entire episode wherein he exclaimed that the Mormons would exterminate the gentiles. A war did ensue in which an extermination order was given that was however; a tongue in cheek expression aimed at ridiculing Rigdon's utterance. This order has been recanted in recent years!]*

Atrocities were committed on both sides. As a part of the peace settlement, the Mormons were required to leave Missouri and Joseph Smith was jailed. Smith later bribed an escape. After the failed attempt on Boggs, Smith's status as a fugitive from justice came into question hastening a series of events which took his life. The arrogance of Smith as a self-deluded "vice-regent of Christ on Earth" is perpetuated in the present church leadership. As such, they justify assassination of character or acts of murder to protect the sanctity of their delusion.]

Once Young was established in Utah, Orrin Porter Rockwell was his chief enforcer bullying and taking lives as necessary to keep the "prophet" in power. He was a dutiful soldier.

224

There was no doubt about my naïveté as I had commenced activity several years earlier. I had believed that which I had been taught as a youngster. However, as my mission progressed, it became obvious that I had to grow out of that naiveté. Challenging each step in each direction I was led, did that.

The contact by John H. Meier in late 1977 came as a surprise. I had heard of him through Preston Truman. Therefore, it was with some interest when he called to pay his respects for my taking the Mormon Church to court. He referred to the "things" the Mormons had done to Howard Hughes. He knew how "sinister" they were.

John had been what he termed a "Scientific Advisor" to Hughes. He had some basics in computer technology in the very early days of mainframe hardware. That marketable skill attracted him to Howard Hughes.

He apparently wore many different hats while employed by Hughes. Among these were handling sensitive matters of political interest to Hughes such as keeping Richard Nixon's brother, Donald out of the public limelight when Nixon was facing some of his first problems over illegal campaign fund raising. Another was attempting to get the Atomic Energy Commission to stop nuclear testing in Nevada.

Still another was his acting as a purchase agent for Hughes in the acquisition of old Nevada gold mining sites. Hughes sought these to chemically reprocess the tailings for recovery of gold. It was this last activity which became the basis for a lawsuit by Summa Corporation against Meier in early 1971, several months after Hughes had been kidnapped out of the Desert Inn casino in Las Vegas.

The lawsuit named nine defendants, one of whom was a resident of Utah. Because of that, the case was filed in Utah District Federal Court. After all defendants had been served, each was dismissed out of the lawsuit except Meier. This left John alone in Utah District Court facing Mormon Judge Aldon Anderson. The suit alleged that Meier had personally profited from the sale of worthless mining sites to Hughes.

After the death of Hughes was reported on April 5th 1976, Mexican police stormed the Hughes penthouse in Acapulco, where they caught the Mormon Mafia shredding thousands of documents. The remaining documents were seized and taken to Mexico City.

Later, a Member of Parliament (MP) in Delta, B.C sent his secretary to Mexico where she made Xerox type copies of about four thousand of those documents. These she took back to Canada. They were perused in an attempt to learn by what means or methods, the Mormon Mafia had been able to bring Hughes into Vancouver after the kidnapping but without taking him through customs or immigration.

Finding nothing of interest to him, the MP turned the papers over to John in the event; he might be able to use them in his defense in Utah.

As a result, John's LA attorney introduced into the court record, a copy of a Hughes penthouse memo which inferred Judge Aldon Anderson was in the "pocket" of the Mormon Mafia and would be used to teach Meier and Bob Maheu a lesson.

Judge Anderson, without any kind of handwriting expert, immediately declared the document a forgery and sealed the record. Later, John would be arrested in Delta, B.C. by Canadian police on a warrant out of Utah alleging obstruction of justice. The treaty between Canada and the U.S. did not provide for extradition on these charges, but some strings were pulled to allow for it. After a long period of incarceration in Canada without bail, the Canadian appellate court ruled that Canada was still a civilized country and a man was presumed innocent until proven guilty.

It was during that time of John's being free on bail before his extradition hearings, that I made the quick visit to him on Halloween, 1978. It was also at that time when, upon returning to Shelton, Marion told me of the effort to involve him in moving drugs, but only after it had been determined he was still my friend.

I did call John about it and he did make contact with the FBI as proven by the telephone call I had from the Seattle office the next day.

The reader will recall my having made a trip to Canada in March of 1978 when John Meier gave me the four thousand documents from the Hughes Penthouse. I had made an earlier trip to meet John in January that year. It turned out I had been tailed by the FBI. After returning, John called me to let me know that FBI agents had gone to the MP in Delta to alert him that John had dealings with a nutty character by the name of Doug Wallace.

The FBI agent in LA, with whom I later had dealings, was, according to John, the same agent who had been to Delta to warn the MP about my involvement with John. I can believe that since the agent, "Richard Garbutte" told me he was doing all he could to keep John out of the Utah District court. In reality, that agent was Richard Bretzing* SAC of the LA office and later head of Mormon Church Security.

[* In January 1979, after I had argued my case in Utah Supreme Court, I traveled to Los Angeles in the company of Mike Culliton. At the building next door to the FBI office on Wilshire Blvd., I made a telephone call to Garbutte. I told him where I was and that I wanted to come over to see him. He panicked at the idea and stammering said he had to go out on a stake out and couldn't possibly meet with me. That confirmed my suspicions about him.]

In their usual manner of indirect attack, The Mormon Danites did a credibility assault on John's Vancouver defense attorney*. When speaking to the Delta MP later, he told me that it was an unconscionable thing that had been done to John's attorney.

[*This was one example of the use of building dossiers on individuals for purposes of discredit by way of use of the BEE lapel pin. More about this later.]

To what extent that discredit played a role in influencing the B.C. court to extradite John to Utah is not known. However, John was extradited.

Jim Barber was selected as John's Utah attorney. At this time, I had moved to Nevada. Jim flew to Reno accompanied by Preston Truman to discuss John's case with me. At that meeting, I told Barber I would like to file a lawsuit in Washington, D.C. on behalf of John alleging a conspiracy by the Mormon Church and the Justice Department against John. He approved of it and I later did so but without success. I had sent out a press release at the time of filing however no media picked up on it. Yet about three weeks later, on the morning that John's case went to the jury, The Salt Lake Tribune Newspaper carried front-page news about my lawsuit. It appeared to be timed to influence the jury.

John was convicted and sentenced to thirty months in federal prison. Later Barber and I had a heated exchange on the telephone. He accused me of having timed my lawsuit to influence the jury. I explained the timing of the publicity was on the part of the Tribune not me. I asked him if he polled the jury about the article before the case was submitted to it. He had failed to do so, which caused me to believe he had been neutralized by the Danites. Had he polled the jury there would likely have been a mistrial.

Before the actual trial in SLC, I had a visit at my office in Carson City by two FBI agents. One of them I knew as a local agent the other introduced himself as being stationed in Las Vegas. They wanted to talk to me about the John Meier case. I excused myself for the morning but asked them to return in the afternoon.

While they were absent, I called Jim Barber. I explained the situation to him. He used some expletives and told me that agent was a SLC agent not Las Vegas. He also said the agent," was as dishonest as a corkscrew and would, "screw his own mother into the ground."

When they returned to my office, I had a tape recorder which I placed in operation. I told them I would not interview without it. They said it was unfair they didn't have one. "Just ask me for a copy", I retorted. I then explained to the agent from "Vegas" that I had checked on him and that he had lied to me.

Initially the government had filed two charges against John. One was for conspiracy to obstruct justice the other was forgery to obstruct justice. Since conspiracy requires the involvement of two or more persons, I anticipated the purpose for the visit was to establish my complicity.

Preston Truman had released certain of the Hughes documents to the students who ran the Utah Daily Chronicle, the newspaper, published by the University of Utah. The students had made hay of those papers which placed Judge Anderson in a bad light. Any connection to me in those publications would have been the nexus to establish conspiracy. After I fully explained that Preston was his own agent to do with the documents as he saw fit, no connection could be made. Because of that interview, the government dismissed the conspiracy charge against John.

Barber had attempted by motion to obtain an order of the court for the Internal Revenue Service (IRS) to produce their microfilm of the same Hughes papers. The IRS had gone to Mexico City and microfilmed those papers. After John was convicted, the IRS microfilm appeared. Preston Truman was appointed as a Hughes expert by the court to take custody of the film to review it to see if the "Pocket" memo was included.

Preston discovered the memo was present in exactly the same format in the microfilm*, as John's attorney had introduced into the court record of the Summa case. This being so, there was no forgery and no obstruction of justice. Based upon that finding, Barber made a motion for a new trial. That motion was denied. Therefore, John served 30 months jail time as a political prisoner of the corrupt agenda of Mormon Church using agents within the federal government both in the Justice Department and the Court within Utah.

The Canadian government sought and obtained the release of John to its custody for the last year of his incarceration. John had not been humbled however and spoke of his exposing the Mormon corruption in the Hughes affairs.

Therefore in the mid 80's John was again arrested on charges of murder and extradited to California where he again was jailed without bail. Eventually, the charges were dismissed and he was released. Nonetheless, John had been discredited by well over fifteen years of unwarranted legal assault both civil and criminal.

As I came to know John, I developed the impression that he was somewhat of a flake making assertions, which he either failed to support, or was unable to support. He was interested more in promoting his own interests than assisting me in my endeavors. I was led to believe John had secreted several file cabinets of information indicting the Mormon Mafia in its dealings with Hughes. It appeared as though the Mormon Mafia made the assault on John because it feared he did indeed have evidence against them.

At this time I have no reason to think that John does indeed possess documentation to establish Bill Gay's take over of Hughes and his empire for purposes of skimming it for the benefit of the Mormon Agenda. If he does, God willing they will yet come forward at a future time.

In 1995, the story of John's trouble was published in a book AGE OF SECRETS written by Vancouver Sun reporter, Gerald Bellett. I received from John advance copy #91 of 100 to the friends of John. I took exception to an attack on me by the author appearing on page 198

In three paragraphs, the author asserts that because of my activities, Judge Anderson came down against John finding him responsible for 7.9 million in damages to Summa Corporation. He also asserted that John tried to keep me from involving him in my fight against the Mormon Church. Such of course was false, as it was John who contacted me with offers of help.

I called John and strongly objected to the assault on me. He responded by saying he didn't know Bellet had said those things. I threatened a lawsuit against him, Bellet and the publisher.

After some discussion with the publisher, I concluded that I would not take action. Certainly the publisher was not liable.

Neither was the author for he only reported what he had been told. Furthermore, except for the reference to my publication, the Millennial Messenger, Doug Wallace could have been any one of the one hundred plus Doug Wallaces listed in U.S. telephone directories.

I cannot blame John for attempting to recoup some of his losses by selling AGE OF SECRETS. Certainly he is entitled to compensation for the years of false imprisonment: loss of consortium; destruction of his business and reputation and loss of years of association with his children.

I did take one other exception to assertions in the book. John claimed that he had viewed the frozen* body of Hughes in a warehouse on an island in the Caribbean.

[Hughes was claimed to have had an interest in kryonics (freezing of his body) in order to preserve it until such time that medical science will have advanced to where he could be thawed out and medically healed to live an indeterminable length of time.]*

Movie actress Terry Moore made a claim on the estate of Hughes alleging she had been secretly married to Hughes on a ship offshore of the United States. She was given a settlement probably more due to the nuisance value of the claim than the merit.

I visited her at home in Santa Monica in September of 1978. Her psychic had told her Hughes' body was in a cold mountain probably in Alaska. I had my own psychic impressions and agreed the body was in a cold mountain however it was in the Rocky Mountains* of Utah not Alaska.

*[*In early 1970, the Mormon Church stopped guided tours of the public through its genealogical vaults in little Cottonwood Canyon, southeast of SLC. It was claimed germs were being introduced which was harmful to the microfilm records being stored there. Simultaneously, they began excavation of another short vault to the west of the main entrance. By Thanksgiving Day 1970, they had completed the new vault equipped with refrigeration. It was on Thanksgiving Day that Hughes was kidnapped out of the Desert Inn in Las Vegas.]*

A question arose in the late seventies as to why former members of the Mormon Mafia (Hughes aides) were on constant vigil at the site of the new vault. Another interesting question can be asked as to why a young black undercover agent for the SLCPD* blew himself up in his car just outside that same vault?

*[*This agent had attempted to infiltrate Preston Truman's employment scene and was discovered. That followed the same attempt by a young 23 year-old white agent. After he was discovered and discharged, he reported to the SLCPD station. He was reported in the newspaper to have had a heart attack while there and was taken out dead. This fits the pattern established of eliminating those who have been exposed and who know too much.]*

Chapter Thirty Four

The Cherry Processor

Sometime after the church changed its posture regarding Black priesthood, I had a contact from Garn Baum who lived in Provo, Utah. I had clipped an article out of the newspaper a year or two earlier, which mentioned his lawsuit against the church. He claimed he had been a victim of anti-trust laws in his fruit processing business.

He called me from Provo and asked if he could meet me. He said he and his wife, Peggy, would drive up from Utah. Since I was working on Don Benson's house in the Shelton area, I suggested he and his wife get a room at the Tyee Motor Lodge in Tumwater. That was the same location I had the TV interview with Seattle's Mormon owned channel 5 KIRO on June 9th.

I drove over to meet them at the Tyee one morning in the fall of 1978. Garn was a tall, slender "cowboy" kind of man. Peggy was a very pretty, dark haired woman. Then as over the years, Peggy always had a fresh flower blossom in her hair. Garn was quite outspoken while Peggy was very quiet and soft-spoken.

They had sued the church and several other defendants for several million Dollars damages alleging the defendants had orchestrated a conspiracy against their business. It seems that Garn had invented a cherry-pitting machine by which he could produce a practically pit-less cherry pack. His processing plant would operate during the cherry picking season. The processed cherries would be frozen and stored in one huge concrete and cinder-block freezer-warehouse from which they would be shipped by truck to the U. S. Armed Forces and makers of pies and yogurt.

The plant was located just north of Brigham Young University on University Avenue. In 1974, the cherry growers who had been happy for years past to sell their fruit to Garn refused to sell to him. A pattern of conspiracy emerged in which the state of Utah

233

Agriculture Department, several growers and the church welfare farm agents appeared to be conspiring to boycott Garn.

There had been some interest on the part of the church to acquire Garn's processing plant for use in the church's own agricultural industry. The church welfare program fronted that industry. Throughout the church, Stakes of the church owned farms on which they produced an agricultural crop. The ostensible use of the crop was for purposes of providing for church members in hard times.

The welfare program became one of the proselytizing tools of the church. It was fashionable for the church to brag on the fact that the church took care of its own. Many converts to Mormonism were attracted more to the welfare program than to the principles of the "gospel". Around the country, you will hear people say, "Well I can't go along with doctrines of Mormonism, but you have to give them credit. They take care of their own."

Go talk to the farmers of Utah, Mormon or non- Mormon and you will find a great deal of unrest. The biggest complaint I have heard is that the church places the surpluses of production from the welfare farms onto the commercial market and thus are in competition with its own member farmers.

The biggest gripe is that the surpluses of the welfare farms were produced on land that is tax exempt* and by labor that is donated. Therefore, a great profit advantage is held by the church over its own members who not only have to pay taxes on property and income but are further expected to donate an additional ten percent of profit as tithing to the church.

[For years it was tax exempt, but in recent years there has been a move around the country to deny tax exempt status.]*

When Garn could not acquire enough fruit, he could not process enough frozen cherries to stay in business. In time, He was not able to make his mortgage payment, and his plant and his home, which was on the property, were sold on the courthouse steps in foreclosure proceedings. The Mormon Church purchased the property at that sale.

At first, Garn attempted to PR his growers offering incentives and higher prices to no avail. Rumors were spread around that Garn would not be able to pay the growers for their fruit and that added to the refusal not to sell to Garn, although he had a contract with a California broker wherein Wells Fargo Bank was furnishing Garn with his operating capital and the growers would be paid for their fruit.

Garn and Peggy had retained an anti-trust attorney in SLC, Dan Berman. A suit was filed in U.S. District Court of Utah. It alleged a conspiracy and sought general and punitive damages. Later, a former partner of Utah Senator, Orrin Hatch, Lowell Summerhays represented them. After a while, Summerhays told the Baums if he pursued their case the way he should, he had reason to believe he would be excommunicated from the Mormon Church. When Summerhays no longer represented the Baums, in order to prosecute the case, they became their own attorney in pro se capacity.

After seeing that I had made inroads into the church by the church reversing itself on Black priesthood, they wanted me to represent them. That was the purpose for the meeting in Tumwater, Washington. After listening to their story and all the very familiar events of church manipulations going on in my current scene in Shelton, I was interested in helping them. There was however, a problem in that I was not licensed in Utah. Although the case was in federal court, federal courts only allow attorneys admitted in the state of their District to practice in their courts.

The Baums had not been able to go forward and the court told them to get an attorney. They told the court they had asked many attorneys in the state to represent them and had been refused. The judge then told them he would accept any attorney from any state to represent them in his court as long as that attorney had been admitted to federal practice.

Before this time, the Baums and their attorney had been successful in removing Aldon Anderson as the judge on the basis he was a Mormon and was prejudiced. A District Court Judge from Denver, Colorado, John Kane was assigned to the case.

I made application to that Judge to be able to represent Garn and Peggy but only as co-counsel. The judge gave me that permission. I was still having some reservations about getting involved due to distance and going through the difficulties, I was having in Shelton.

However, as the situation there began to wind down, I decided to make a trip to Provo for a final decision on whether I would make a formal appearance in the case. So during the first week of December 1978, I went to Provo and then to the court in SLC. I decided to enter the case and filed a formal appearance.

Later, the out of state Judge got out of the case and a new Judge, Bruce Jenkins, was assigned. He was a Mormon so I filed a motion of disqualification. He refused to remove himself.

I traveled to Provo several times during the first part of 1979 to attend hearings on motions made in that case and once to participate in a deposition of certain of the defendants. It began to appear to me that the cards were stacked against the Baums.

On one occasion, I was given a one-day notice by the court clerk of a hearing for summary judgement. Counsel for the Church had failed to give me the required 5-day notice. In fact, he had failed to give me any notice. Because of that, I had the clerk issue summonses to several top leaders of the church. I served the summonses before noon on the day of the hearing for appearances at 1:30PM.

At the hearing, a number of defendants with high priced attorneys appeared with motions to suppress the summonses. At that hearing it was brought out that I had not been given proper notice of the hearing. One of the junior grade members of a large firm was made the scapegoat and the court postponed the hearing.

That was the last time I appeared in court with the Baums. At the next hearing, the court granted the defendant's motion for summary judgment thus dismissing the case. The Baums filed an appeal but the dismissal of the lower court was upheld by the Tenth Circuit.

An effort had been made to get this story on CBS' "60 Minutes" television news show. I traveled to Provo for the interview with producers Roz Carson of Los Angeles and Dick Clark of New York. Harry Reasoner, the interviewer, was supposed to have been there but I was told he was in recovery from an alcohol binge.

I remember sitting around the kitchen table in the Baums home with Roz and Dick. I remember Dick telling about his childhood on a farm. He spoke of rabbit hunting with a ferret. "When you put the ferret down a rabbit burrow, it was just a matter of time before a rabbit would come popping out somewhere. We'll do that with this segment of 60 minutes", he had said

They had of course made contact with the church and had been taken around to several church welfare farms and been given some church indoctrination. They had also been given an audio cassette tape of a conversation between two Mormons about me. Neither Roz nor Dick would give me the tape or allow me to listen to it. They claimed it was slanderous and did not want to involve CBS or 60 Minutes in a lawsuit.

In December 1979, the 60 Minutes segment was aired. The church reeled under public airings of an assertion of wrong doing by the church leadership and a conspiracy between it, the Utah Department of Agriculture and several cherry growers.

The church went on the warpath. They were able to obtain a retraction on the part of Harry Reasoner who said that it was the worst piece of journalism he had ever been involved with. Dick Clark lost his job at 60 Minutes, went on to work for 20/20 for awhile. He later died under mysterious circumstances. Roz Carson drew back in her shell and would not respond to my communications to her.

This is an example of the economic power of the Mormon Church in this day and age. The church owned station in SLC, KSL, is an affiliate of CBS. Being a subordinate affiliate one would wonder how they were able to pull it off. Yet, the truth goes to the reality of the extent of Mormon influence in commercial advertising not just by church owned businesses, but to businesses presided over by Mormon executives.

This economic power is constantly demonstrated not only in SLC but also throughout Utah. Newspapers do not stay in business from income of subscribers. It is the income from advertising, which brings a profit. Dry up advertising and you dry up income. That is why boycotting is such an effective tool in manipulating the press. TV stations in Utah are likewise faced with limitations in their public airing of criticisms of the Mormon Church.

The church owned Deseret Newspaper and its ostensible rival, The Salt Lake Tribune, long ago made a pact for economic survival of the Tribune. Because of that pact, both papers share a common advertising agency. And because of that pact, the Tribune can go only so far in publishing news items or letters to the editor critical of the Mormon Church.

Economic boycotting is not limited to Utah. Indeed, anywhere the church has a population base, it is a tool to prevent truth embarrassing to the church* from being published. In such a clime, it could be said that freedom of the press is an illusion, having sold its independence for naught but money.

[* This issue is the reason behind the church having established its Public Communications Department. It places a local censorship office of the church in major cities of the world through which all news items affecting the church may be cleared for publication. The other job of the Public Communications Department is to keep adverse news items local.]

Garn was quite hard headed about his situation. He had been raised to respect and honor the right thing. Both he and Peggy were Mormon, that is they had been raised in the church having gone through the usual rote training of children. They followed what they understood to be "right".

As is the case in Utah, so many members of the church take the church for granted. That is especially true of members in the outlying areas such as farmers. Sunday is church going time but the rest of the week one is supposed to work. Garn had been raised on that work ethic.

When the Boycott of his business began he found it very difficult to believe the Church, his church, would be involved in doing such a thing to him. When it became clear that it was, he never hesitated to speak directly to church leaders telling them what he thought about the situation and what they should do about it.

His entire life became obsessed with the injustice he was suffering from the church. The church owed him for what it had done to him and there was no way that a manipulated federal court system could prove to him that the church was not involved or that it did not owe him.

He refused for a long time to seek outside employment to provide income for him and Peggy. Siblings and close friends assisted them as much as they could. According to Peggy, early in the case President N. Eldon Tanner stated his intention to make a settlement with Garn. Tanner told church attorney, Wilford Kirton to, "Make it right* with this man" (Garn Baum) but Kirton never made it right.

[According to Garn and Peggy, a few years later, Elder Gordon B. Hinckley (Most recent past President of the Mormon Church) offered Garn a $5 million loan to get Garn to drop the church from the lawsuit. Hinckley said that Garn would have to take $900.000.00 off the top of the$5 million and repay the church for the cost of their purchasing Garn's property and expenses Hinckley said had incurred since the purchase. Garn refused the $5 million; he didn't want a LOAN! Later, Bishop Richard Losee told Garn he wouldn't have to pay it back. Garn said that was different and asked was Hinckley's offer still good. Losee said he would see and arranged a meeting with himself, Hinckley and Garn. Hinckley told Garn at that meeting he intended to do nothing for him, as they (Hinckley and the church hierarchy) believed they could "whip" him.]*

Garn was hard headed, but he was also a man of extremely high moral fiber. A giant of morality standing taller than any of the Mormon leaders.

Garn and Peggy filed a common law lien on their property to prevent the church from evicting them. By this means, they were able to remain in possession of the property until one morning in August 1985 when Garn had gone out for his usual morning

239

breakfast. At seeing him leave the property a number of armed men minutes later came surrounding the house.

Peggy was escorted off the property and when Garn came back from breakfast, armed men refused him admittance to the property. The church made arrangements at a hotel for temporary accommodations for Peggy and Garn. Their furniture and personal possessions were taken to a storage unit and they were never allowed back on the property. Since the Baums were not able to afford to store their possessions, they later picked up a few things. However, everything had been jammed into the storage space and it was difficult to find specific items. However, most of the possessions were never recovered and they were sold off at public auction.

For those who believe the fiction that the church president, his counselors and the "Apostles" are men of God, heirs to leading the "Kingdom" of God on earth, this outrageous example of lack of humanity should be an eye opener. They can have all the statutes of a gentle Jesus adorning their visitor's center they want, what they do bespeaks who they are.

Garn sought employment with the U.S. Forest Service where he worked during the summer months. He did this for a number of years well into his 70's. He was in charge of designing and building a truck-cradle in which the people's national Christmas tree rode to Washington, D.C., for 1996--Utah's Centennial Tree--1896-1996. Garn took ill and passed away in May 1999. His wife Peggy survives and is completing her writings on the tribulations she and Garn went through in their struggle against the unethical conduct of the Mormon Church.

In the end, the church failed in its quest to acquire Garn's invention. He had removed it long before the church swept in and took possession of the property. The property has never been used for the processing of any kind of agriculture products. Before the church took it over the property had been a productive part of the county tax rolls afterwards and to this day, [1999] it is not.

It has been sad to drive by the property and see it not operating as it was in the days before the church and a few others orchestrated the conspiracy to boycott Garn and Peggy's business. I have regretted that I was not able to help them more than I did. Unfortunately, they fell victim to the pervasive power in Utah.

Chapter Thirty Five

More Intrigue

For a number of years, the presiding judge of the Utah federal District Court was a former University of Utah law professor, Willis Ritter. Judge Ritter had a reputation for being cantankerous and not giving the Mormon Church an inch of unjustified or illegal leeway in its prosecution or defense of lawsuits.

Judge Ritter was not a Mormon but had lived most of his life in Utah and was well aware of the agenda of the church. His life had been threatened many times because of his posture of non-favoritism to the church. Because of that, he had a security guard of U.S. Marshals to protect him around the clock.

In January 1978, Newsweek Magazine featured a picture of him on its front cover. In the article inside, he was attributed as having had the strength and moral fiber to support and re-enforce the law of equal justice in his court. The article referred to the times he would not give special privileges to Mormon interests. He was reported to be a cantankerous individual and many complaints were heard concerning his administration of the court. While a lot of the complaints had merit he was most despised because of his attitude toward the Mormon Church.

Judge Ritter followed in the tradition of earlier federal judges who had been assigned to the territory of Utah. One in particular was associate justice John Cradlebaugh who on the 8th of March 1859 traveled to Provo to hold a term of the court. Alexander Wilson was the prosecuting attorney and Peter Dodson, marshal. Because of the enmity between the appointed federal court and the Mormons, Two light companies of artillery escorted the judge.

Judge Cradlebaugh empanelled a grand jury to investigate the Parrish-Potter homicide of March 14, 1857. In empanelling the jury, Cradlebaugh issued the following instructions:

"You are the tools, the dupes,

the instruments of tyrannical

church despotism.

You are taught to obey

orders and to commit horrid

crimes. Deprived of your liberty,

you have lost your manhood

and become the willing

instruments of bad men. I say

unto you, it will be my earnest

effort while among you to

knock off your ecclesiastical

shackles

and set you free."

(A History of Springville page 33)

The jury was to investigate the Parrish-Potter murders also known as the "Springville murders". It was rumored that Parrish wanted to get out of the territory and move to California. He knew too much about how Brigham Young ruled the territory. It was feared his information would further inflame gentile (Non Mormon) sentiments against the church and he was murdered under the Blood Atonement doctrine of the church.

In keeping with the enmity against federal control of Utah, Judge Ritter was pronounced dead less than two weeks after his picture was on the cover of Newsweek. Any excuse that he died of natural causes is dispelled when one considers the next national event to occur.

About two weeks after Judge Willis Ritter's picture was on the cover of Newsweek, another enemy of the church was featured on the Newsweek cover. This was John Singer, an acknowledged fundamentalist of Mormonism. He had been excommunicated from the church. John practiced polygamy having three wives. He had been at odds with the Utah education Department over his insistence that his children be educated at home. That was the thrust of the accompanying article in Newsweek. Less than two weeks later, John Singer was dead from a shotgun blast to his back

John and Vickie Singer in 1978

He had gone to his mailbox and was confronted by police. They had a warrant for his arrest for failure to obey a court order instructing him to show cause why he should not be held in contempt of court for failure to place his children in the public school system.

Singer turned to walk away and was shot in the back with a 12 gauge shot gun. He died instantly. Later his legal wife, Vicky, asked a Mormon medical doctor to view the remains at the mortuary. That doctor did so and reported to her that Singer had what appeared to be a shot gun wound in his back.

For doing that, the doctor and his wife were both excommunicated from the church. The grounds were, "Cavorting with a known excommunicant of the church." I received a copy of the doctor's story and a plea to help him if I could. Unfortunately, I had already discovered that civil courts will not interfere with the proceedings of a church tribunal.

Thus we had two deaths of national figures within two weeks of each other and in each case; opposition to Mormon Church rules was at issue. Further, their story reached national scope by their pictures on the cover of a National magazine. This fact should have given rise to a federal investigation for violations of civil rights. However, since the federal government in Utah is under control of the Mormon Church, that was never done.

In Oregon in the spring of 1978, a large controversy appeared in the newspapers over mysterious microwaves. It seemed that the microwave transmissions were evident in the Willamette valley. There was concern that these transmissions would be harmful to children. Some 25 individuals were complaining of ringing in their ears and of headaches.

There had been earlier reports in the media of microwave transmissions bombarding the American Embassy in Moscow. Children of embassy officials had been sent back to the United States for medical check ups. There were never any reports of harmful effects of the radiation. It was because of that Soviet bombardment that the concerns, especially in the Eugene, Oregon area, were considered.

Many theories about the source of the radiation were put forth. One was that it was coming off high voltage transmission power lines in Texas. That theory said the radiation was bouncing off the atmosphere and returning to earth in the Willamette Valley of Oregon. Later that theory was debunked.

The Environmental Protection Agency (EPA) was brought into the act. According to its investigation, The Naval Air Station at Alameda California was the culprit. The University of Oregon's Industrial hygienist, Marshall Van Ert, took exception to that theory since the Naval Station broadcast at 4.71 megahertz and the mysterious signal was at 4.75 megahertz with 1,100 vibrations per second.

Scientists at Portland's Tektronix also took exception to the EPA finding. According to Clifford Shrock, spectrum analysis specialist at Tektronix who was retained to make a study of the signals, the signals were very strong and he would not rule out that they were coming from outer space.

The reader will remember my dialogue with my father in the spring of 1975 that the BEE lapel pin was activated by a radio signal. At his request, I told him there was a hole in the system in the Willamette Valley and that the church had to install a booster station to obtain full coverage. I further identified the location of the booster station as in the Estacada-Redlands area of Oregon.

The reader will also remember that I had been the victim of eavesdropping by that system at least four times. Once when in Salt Lake City at church headquarters conversing with D. Arthur Haycock in the spring of 1975, another time when Roy King and his son-in-law came into my home in January 1976 attempting to find out what I was up to and then next day when my ex-wife Pat was wearing it to find out what the Home Teachers could not the day before. Finally when set up for the interview with "Brother Ashton" in the church tower on April 6, 1976.

The "official" EPA finding put an end to further inquiry regarding the mysterious signals affecting the Willamette Valley. If what I had said was true three years earlier, then the EPA finding was a cover-up of the truth. This should be a scary situation for all Americans, that the heads of governmental agencies owe an allegiance to the Mormon prophet greater than allegiance to the American people. When the truth is known that the Mormon Church has been working for years to place it's agents within the Federal government in positions at high levels, it is indeed scary.

It was not until the spring of 1979 that I learned exactly what the BEE lapel pin system was all about. I attended a seminar in Houston Texas on the subject of electronic surveillance. Police Chiefs from all over the United States attended. The more usual methods of wire-tapping and planted bugs were discussed at great length. On the 2nd day of the seminar, I asked the instructor what was the most sophisticated technology for spying then available.

His response was that there were two systems. The first was called laser bounce. In this system, a beam of laser is aimed at a window in the target building. The laser is then bounced off to a receiver at a remote location. Persons speaking within the room, at which the laser is aimed, vibrate the glass in the window. The vibrations on the glass then alter the frequency of the laser beam so that when it reached the receiver, they have a modulated laser beam. It then becomes a simple matter to remove the frequency of the laser leaving vibration of the window glass. This can be reduced to sound much as was the system used by the old Gramophone. However, the system relies on precise alignment of the laser beam and the signal and can be very difficult to set up and maintain.

The other system and the most sophisticated is the microwave Cavity resonator. In this system, a target is bombarded with microwave signals. Within the target area is located a cavity resonator. The cavity resonator is a mini sized windowpane, which vibrates with the audible sounds within its range. For purposes of spying, the audible sounds would be conversations between persons.

Like in the laser bounce system, the microwaves are merged with the audio vibrations into a modulated signal, which can be received anywhere. The known radio frequency is removed leaving pure audio.

According to the instructor at the surveillance seminar, only entities with unlimited capital could afford the microwave Cavity Resonator system due to its expensive nature. When Mormon Bill Gay had control of Hughes assets, he created, Hughes Teledynamics for the express purpose of creating for the Mormon Church the BEE lapel pin (cavity resonator) and all the other expensive electronic equipment needed to support the system. It was that equipment which found its way to the top floors of the Mormon Tower in Salt Lake City, Utah.

To what extent the Federal government is involved in the conspiracy for Mormons to "save the Constitution" and take control of the world for the Mormon President, "Earth King" is unknown. However, it can be established that Mormon agents within the various agencies of the government are daily at work doing the bidding of the Mormon "Prophet".

In this book I have connected dots between psychic events and happenings to demonstrate the power of the Cosmos in informing persons gifted with the sensitivity of paranormal precognition and even retro-cognition of events.

While I sought investigation of the John Ragan murder, no agency of state or Federal government would investigate. Therefore what I have written is a personal indictment of the events and perpetrators based upon "seeing" the event approximately one week before it happened together with six months of collateral events openly transpiring.

There is no statute of limitations for murder and unless the government investigates and establishes the facts as I have outlined them the murder will go uninvestigated and the perpetrators unpunished.

Chapter Thirty Six

Ending the First Fifty Years

In May 1980 I turned 51 years of age. My initial battle with the church beginning in 1976 had yielded the formal abolishment of Black racism as far as the restriction on priesthood was concerned. Little more had been accomplished. However, I would continue to bark at the heels of church leadership without any marked success.

My dilemma, which had me thinking that God wanted more out of me than that seemed to prove otherwise at least for the moment. I had envisioned the accomplishment of far greater feats but they would be far off into the future if indeed they materialized at all.

As I write these words it is January 2001 nearly twenty six years since the ordination of Larry Lester. I have constantly postured myself to be prepared to do the will of God when the timing has been shown to me. I have not pursued material things. I have helped others to achieve their financial goals but have not for myself.

I have pondered why so much happened in the first few years after my November 1st 1975 decision to follow the promptings I would receive and yet nothing of significance has occurred. I recall Betty Moretti telling me from her insight that it would be many years before further significant developments would occur, in fact she said, "About thirty years".

I began writing this book in the winter of 1998-99. I have determined to publish it on the Internet to allow as many people to become aware of what I experienced and to gain some insight into the sinister nature of the Church of Jesus Christ of Latter Day Saints (LDS Church) more commonly known as the Mormon Church.   February 2001

Epilogue

I posted this book on the internet in February 2001 but took it down in January 2005 for reasons I will describe in the next book.

In March and May of 2009, I was twice taken to emergency for sudden low blood pressure. After a clean bill of health with all vital signs normal both times I awakened to the fact that at age 80 I was likely having conscience attacks because I have not actively pursued the original mandate given me. Because of this and the update concerning discoveries of proven paranormal experiences made in the forward to this book I feel I am obliged at this late age to again be embarked on the mission with scientific approval of the veracity of events that had previously driven me. However in some strange way beginning in December 2007, I have written open letters to the LDS Hierarchy explaining that some events to negatively affect them were in the offing. They of course continue to hide in their bubble of silence.

It now appears that the second part of the mission includes establishing equality among members of the church regardless of gender or sexual orientation of church members as the church has a war going against gays and lesbians which God seems to want ended. I am again engaging in that noble struggle. In addition, I am open to whatever may be required of me by the Cosmos which will likely be concerned with the abatement of any effort by the Mormon Church or any other group of conspirators to create a one world government of fascism as told me on May 8th 1937. In this latter effort I seek the association of those persons who have a sense of calling from a higher source and who feel they have been encouraged over their lifetime to study and discover the answers for the extreme problems both political and financial that presently face the world.

August 27, 2009

Nov 17, 2012 last editing . New Cover May, 2015

Notes:

Notes:

Made in the USA
San Bernardino, CA
29 May 2015